The Adventures of
Bruno

First published 2021

Published under licence by Brown Dog Books and
The Self-Publishing Partnership Ltd, 10b Greenway Farm, Bath Rd,
Wick, nr. Bath BS30 5RL

www.selfpublishingpartnership.co.uk

ISBN printed book: 978-1-83952-356-4

Cover design by Andrew Prescott
Internal design by Andrew Easton
Photographs by Annie Jones
Illustrations by Emily Grundy

Credits: p15 image: Antony Gormley, ANOTHER PLACE, 1997
Cast iron 189 x 53 x 29 cm (100 elements)
Permanent installation, Crosby Beach, Merseyside, England
© the artist

Printed and bound in the UK

This book is printed on FSC certified paper

The Adventures of Bruno

Bruno and Milly in Lockdown Land

Annie Jones & Emily Grundy

BROWN
DOG
BOOKS

Contents

This is Bruno

This is Bruno:

As you can see, Bruno is a dog – a Border Terrier, the best of dogs (in Bruno's opinion and in mine). Border Terriers used to be called Coquetdale Terriers, because their origins lie in the rough wild country of the Coquetdale region of Northumberland. Does Bruno have some ancestral memory of this, I sometimes wonder? He loves the beaches and countryside walks of Northumberland and seems very at home in that dog-friendly area when we go on holiday there.

Bruno lives with me in our house near Manchester, in the north of England. My Jack Russell terrier, Milly, lives here too. (Jack Russells are also the best of dogs, of course). She can be a bit of a diva sometimes, but Bruno is very patient with her (until he isn't). He never growls or bites, but he might, just sometimes and not very often, look at her in a certain way. I'm not sure what message is being conveyed, but the effect on Milly is that she leaves the food, or toy or place on the chair and retreats to the conservatory. Tired from the effort of disciplining Milly, Bruno usually goes to sleep at this point. Job done.

Bruno is on the big side for a Border Terrier, with long legs and a shaggy coat. He is wheaten in colour, and people often say he looks like a teddy bear, particularly when he is ready to have his regular haircut. He turned ten a month ago, which would be very young if he were a human being but is kind of middle aged for a Terrier. If he were a bigger dog, like a Labrador, say, he would be quite old at ten – bigger dogs tend to have shorter lives. But Terriers can live to 15 or 16, so with luck he will be around for a few years yet. It's hard to imagine a world without Bruno (though maybe Milly doesn't find it quite as hard to imagine as I do).

Bruno is a character. He has his own way of thinking about things and his own way of doing things. He knows what he likes – furry cushions, big dog beds, radiators, little bone-shaped dog treats, chasing ducks and squirrels, countryside walks and beaches. He likes his meals at regular times, plenty of treats, and playing 'Chase'. A favourite game is hiding Milly's toy, and then watching her search for it. You can see him smile when she fails to find it. Bruno was also quite smitten by the white and fluffy Bichon Frise we used to meet sometimes when walking round the lake, but, sadly for Bruno, she now walks somewhere else, with angel wings.

Bruno knows what he doesn't like, too. He's not keen on change. He's really not keen on Alsatians – he has his reasons. He's not terribly fond of Staffies, either – again he has his reasons. He doesn't like noise, or fireworks, or visitors who stay longer than he considers appropriate. He protests vigorously when I steer the car towards the veterinary surgery where we go to see our vet. He likes our vet, but he has plenty to say if she or the nurse gets out the latex gloves. He does not like veterinary staff wearing latex gloves. He has his reasons for this, too, but they are none of your business. Some things are private.

Bruno and I don't always agree. Maybe we are both becoming more rigid and pernickety as we get older. One of the things about which we disagree is the old red leather settee in our middle room. I like the throw to be placed neatly over the back of the settee, with the cushions artistically arranged across the seat. Bruno disagrees, vigorously. He enlists Milly's help, and they set about rearranging settee, cushions and throw to their own taste.

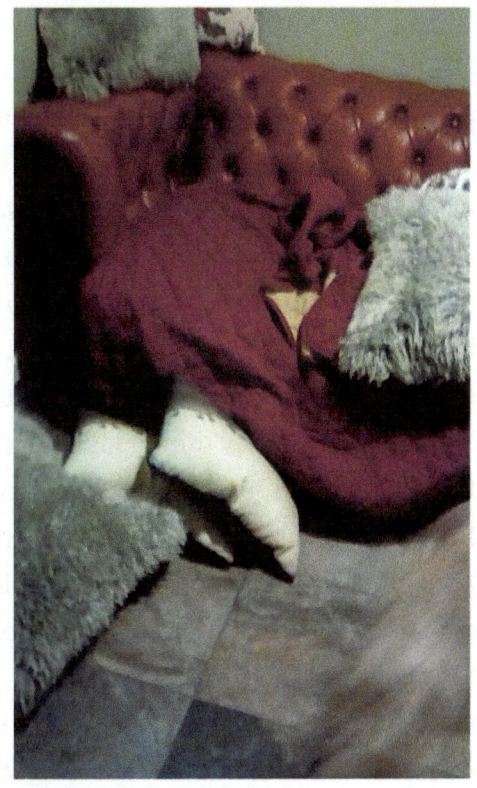

If you look closely, you can just see a little bit of Blurry Bruno in the bottom right-hand corner of the photograph. That's the tail end. The head end is busy pulling more cushions into a heap on the floor. Bruno doesn't understand why I am not pleased with his efforts at interior design. Surely I can see how much better his ideas are than mine?

Sadly, we must agree to disagree. Five times a day, at

least, I pile all the cushions back on to the settee. As soon as I leave the room, Bruno begins the laborious task of getting the cushions back to where they should be – on the floor. Sometimes Milly helps him, and sometimes she has better things to do. It's possible I'm weakening. I looked at the cushions piled on the floor last night – and left them there. Bruno looked so comfortable in the nest he had made. The obvious thing to do, of course, would be to get rid of the cushions. But, like Bruno, I am stubborn and have my own ideas of how things should be. And I like settees to have cushions.

One of Bruno's favourite things to do is weeing on walls, and he is very pernickety about this. There's a lot to say about Bruno and walls, and the best way to wee on them, so we'll come back to it later. He has clear rules for pooping, too. He will never, under any circumstances, poop in his own garden. He will explode first. Other people's gardens are fair game, but his own garden must be poop-free, though he accepts with reluctance that Milly does not share his views. Our vet says that Bruno's refusal to poop in our garden shows that he is a better trainer of human beings than I am of dogs. In refusing to poop in the garden, he ensures that I take him out for a walk at least twice a day, and sometimes thrice. Bruno is really quite clever.

I am sitting at my dining table typing this on my laptop. It is about five minutes before the time that I usually feed Bruno and Milly, but I am still sitting here, rather than sorting out the dogs' dishes in the kitchen. Bruno disapproves of my slowness to tackle the important task of dog feeding. For the last couple of minutes, he has continued to come back and forth to the door, sit with his head on one side, and yip, to remind me what time it is. As I've ignored him, at first he turned his back on me and subsided, grumbling, on to the floor.

The Adventures of Bruno

Border Terriers are good at sulking. I still didn't move, though, so now he's got up and walked over to where I am sitting. He is sitting down by my side by the table, and keeps nudging my leg with his head. 'Get a move on! Where's our dinner? Yip!'

He may not be able to speak, but he can certainly convey a message.

Maybe I should get up and feed him?

Two hours later:

I'm back. Bruno and Milly have been fed. We went for a walk and then played 'Chase' and 'Fetch' in the living room. Bruno likes his squeaky pink elephant, though the squeak no longer works and the elephant's stuffing peeks out from the hole where its leg was before Bruno chewed it off. Milly's favourite toy is her ball. We finally found a ball that Bruno cannot destroy and we are hanging on to it.

Some people would say that I am being anthropomorphic in my descriptions of Bruno and his adventures, ascribing human traits and motivations to doggy behaviours.

And of course I am being anthropomorphic. I am not a dog, and I cannot truly know what the experience of being a dog feels like from the inside. Dogs perceive the world in different ways to us humans. They see colours differently and they take in much more of their information about the world around them through their sense of smell. What I am writing about here is my observations of doggy life from the outside, my imagined version of Bruno's experiences. And, after all, we are all mammals, ultimately descended from a common ancestor. Dogs and humans have shared their lives for many thousands of years. Maybe we are more alike than we might imagine?

Bruno Wees on a Wall

As I've already mentioned, one of Bruno's favourite things to do is to wee against a wall. If there doesn't happen to be a wall nearby, then he will make do with a fence, or a tree, or a gate, or a lamppost, and, ~~once~~, ~~twice~~, three times now – he got a bit muddled up with his aim and weed on my leg. It was an accident. I forgave him – ~~both~~ all three times. But we've had stern words about the fact that my leg is off limits in future, as far as weeing is concerned.

You've probably seen boy dogs weeing against walls and trees and lampposts. They just cock their leg, take aim, and that's that. They might have a sniff round and then move on. Job done.

And it isn't only boy dogs. Milly is a girl, but she often does exactly the same thing – maybe this is her version of girl power?

Bruno watches with some disdain these other dogs who wee on walls. He seems to think that most of them are unacceptably slapdash in their technique. It's not enough just to wee against a wall in any old way. Bruno has to do it PROPERLY. And 'doing it properly' involves a lot of careful thought, planning and practice. For the person at the other end of Bruno's lead (i.e. me) all this can be tedious. But Bruno refuses to be rushed. The rain might be falling in rivers. We might be pelted by hailstones. We might be shivering as the snow falls or trembling as the thunder crashes all around us, but Bruno won't be rushed. Walls are there to be weed on, and this has to be done with exactitude and precision. Bruno is confident that Milly and I understand the importance of accuracy in wall weeing (despite the unfortunate incidents involving my leg and, just once, Milly's head).

Short of picking him up and carrying him – difficult for me because I walk using a walking stick so don't have enough hands – then I just have to be patient. Bruno will wee in his own good time. And then we will walk another two or three feet along the path, until it is time to wee again on the next bit of wall. It can take half an hour or longer to complete the ten-minute walk round the block. Bruno won't move on to the next bit of wall until he is completely satisfied that this bit of wall has been weed on correctly. PROPER wall weeing involves making a careful visual inspection of the wall, and choosing the best brick or stone to aim at. Bruno prepares to wee, then hesitates. He needs to have a good sniff at the wall. He needs to turn around a few times, to make sure he is in the best position to take aim at the chosen brick. But maybe he's chosen the wrong brick? So we have to do it all again with the brick next to the brick first chosen. But perhaps the first one is best after all? So we return to the first brick. Bruno will NOT move on until he is completely satisfied that this bit of wall has been weed on thoroughly and correctly.

I imagine that Bruno can speak. He speaks with a solid, matter of fact Lancashire accent, and he sounds quite a lot like my long dead grandad. 'If a job's worth doing,' he says, 'it's worth doing properly'.

Walls exist to be weed on. And Bruno conveys his certainty that we all owe it to every wall to make sure that they are given the effort and attention they deserve, section by section. Brick by brick. Bruno is no slacker.

Perfectionists like Bruno can sometimes find life difficult. We went to the Kielder Forest in Northumberland once. We'd had quite a long drive, so pulled into one of the picnic areas along the forest road and let the dogs out of the car. Milly toddled off, had a sniff round, and a wee in the grass, and settled down for a drink of water. Bruno looked all around him – ALL THESE TREES! WHERE DO I START? HELP! He was paralysed by all the choice. He turned round and around – hundreds of trees in every direction – and jumped back into the car. He can cope with a small woodland area, but a whole forest was just too much.

Bruno has two ambitions, two items for his bucket list – both, sadly, probably unachievable.

If you've ever been to Crosby, in Merseyside, you will probably have seen Antony Gormley's art installation, *Another Place*. If you haven't seen it, it consists of 100 casts of Antony Gormley's body placed at intervals along the beach and out to sea. It is a strange and haunting sight, well worth a visit. Bruno's ambition is to wee on every single one of the 100 figures.

Sadly, it's an ambition that can never be fulfilled because some of the figures arc too far out to sea to be reached by a little dog, however brave and determined he may be. This won't stop Bruno from trying, though.

His second ambition is something he doesn't like to talk about too much because he doesn't want us to think him big-headed. But he's pretty sure, deep down, that come the day that precision weeing becomes an Olympic event, he would achieve bronze – at least. He had

hoped to have the opportunity to show his talent at the 2020 Olympic Games, but he knows that humans don't share his commitment and drive in this field of endeavour. Maybe one day …

In the meantime, Bruno keeps himself in training every day. Everywhere we go, there are walls to be weed on, and where there are no walls, there are trees. Even at home, Bruno can get in some practice by weeing on the fence, or the shed or the conifers at the end of the garden, where there are enough trees to give him some choice, but not so many that his bladder takes fright. Life is full of opportunity, after all. We've agreed that he will do his absolute best to remember that my leg is not an appropriate target for a wee, and, apart from his ~~second~~ third little slip-up ~~yesterday~~ this morning, he's been very good.

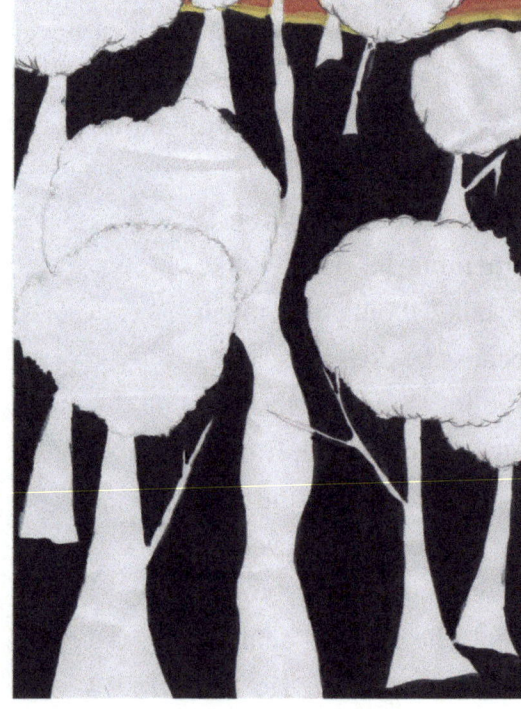

So many trees …
so little time …

Bruno and the Leaves

Of my two dogs, Bruno is almost always the one who has the good ideas. But, just once in a while, my other dog, Milly, can have good ideas, too. Even Bruno admits that.

So, one day, early last autumn, we all went for a walk. It was one of those clear, crisp autumn days, with bright blue skies, and fluffy white clouds and the warning of winter coldness in the air. It was the day to dig out my woolly scarf and gloves, and put on my boots. The previous night had been very windy, and there were piles of newly fallen leaves everywhere, all the colours of autumn heaped up by the path and around the trees.

Milly dived into the leaves at a run, scattering them everywhere, chasing them, jumping up and down on them, seeming to enjoy their papery rustling as she charged through them. If a dog can smile, she was smiling. Bruno sat down patiently at my side as I watched Milly and the leaves. Bruno watched too, his head on one side, but he didn't participate. He seemed quite willing to let Milly have her playtime. But enough is enough. After a few minutes, he shook his lead and barked. 'Come on! Get on with the walk!'

It's possible, though, that an idea had taken root in his furry canine brain.

Leaves. Autumn is full of leaves, everywhere except on the trees. Newly fallen leaves make a sound as you kick your way through them, and you can watch them scatter everywhere. Perhaps this might be fun?

You'll never know if you don't try it, so Bruno decided to give it a go – on every walk for the next couple of weeks. He kicked and rustled his way through every pile of leaves we met – and we met quite a few. What with the precision required for weeing on walls and kicking through leaves, the ten-minute walk round the block now lasted anything up to an hour. An hour's walk round the lake could take all morning.

You have to take your opportunities when they are there, and nothing lasts for ever. After a couple of weeks and a lot of rain, the beautiful, colourful piles of leaves became dark, sodden heaps, and no fun at all. With two dogs, an uneven gait and a walking stick, I picked my way carefully around the piles of dead leaves as they became slippery and treacherous. But we enjoyed the moment whilst it lasted, Milly, Bruno and I, kicking our way through the newly fallen leaves whilst they were fresh and lovely.

And Bruno won't forget. Terriers, like elephants, have long memories. They never forget a friend, or an enemy or a good game, or that there might be sausages in the fridge. The leaves will fall again next autumn, and, when they do, Bruno will be ready to play …

Bruno and the Fox Poo

Do you know what? – I don't think I can bear to describe Bruno's adventure with the fox poo in too much detail. If you've ever had a dog who rolled in fox poo, you will certainly remember the experience without my help. If you haven't, I don't want to upset you with too graphic a description of what happens when one small hairy dog becomes coated with smelly green slime. There may be things in the world that smell worse than fox poo. I'll let you know if I ever find them.

So I'll just give you the highlights. It was a very warm day, the kind of humid, airless day when smells lie heavy in the air. They linger. I'd taken the dogs to the lake in the hope it would be cooler by the water, where we could walk in the shade of the trees. Both dogs were rootling around in the undergrowth by the lakeside – and there it was. A lurking, beckoning pile of fox poo. Sadly, Bruno saw it before I did.

I tried to stop him – trust me, I really tried – but he's a fast mover when he wants to be. I finally caught hold of his collar – but too late. It was an unusually large pile of fox poo, and Bruno is quite a small dog … He achieved good coverage …

We made the Walk of Shame back to the car – did I mention that we were several miles from home, so that it was inevitable that Bruno had to get back into my car? Other, better-behaved dogs made detours to avoid having to get too close to Toxic Bruno, apart, that is, from Ozzie, a scruffy cockapoo, who has his own history of unfortunate encounters with fox poo, horse poo, sheep poo and goose poo. And he doesn't just roll in it. Don't read this next bit if you are prone to queasiness. Ozzie eats it. Even Bruno thinks that is going too far.

Other dog owners expressed their sympathy as we sidled past apologetically. One or two people couldn't avoid displaying just a touch of schadenfreude – thank God it was Bruno, and not Jake or Tilly or Tyson, they were thinking. 'You'll have a job getting Bruno clean again!', laughed the man who walks Bobby, the Jack Russell terrier. Bobby strutted past, tail high, enjoying Bruno's disgrace and his own superior virtue.

We got back to the car eventually. I opened the tailgate. Bruno looked at me with an appeal in his eyes. Wasn't I going to lift him up into the car?

No, I wasn't. I hardened my heart and told him he'd have to jump up under his own steam. No way was I coming into closer contact with him than was necessary. He protested, but eventually accepted the bribe of a dog treat and leapt into the car. I saw the green streaks appear on the dog bed … Bruno saw them, too. He knew, with a sinking heart, that he would be in the shower within two minutes of arriving home.

I drove with all the car windows open. It must have helped a bit. It didn't help much. The smell of fox poo, once encountered, is not forgotten – especially when you smell it on a hot day in a confined space. Bruno didn't seem to mind the smell. He might have been trying to think of ways to avoid the shower …

My first thought, on arriving home, was to put Bruno in the washing machine on a hot wash. My second thought was that perhaps my first thought was a bad idea, tempting though it might be.

My third thought was to put Bruno into the shower and, once my rubber gloves were securely in place, give him a good scrub. Again I don't want to upset you by giving too much detail, but getting fox poo out of Border Terrier hair is no easy task. It's actually quite difficult. It takes effort and commitment and a strong stomach.

'Apply shampoo to wet hair. Work into a lather. Rinse, and repeat if necessary'. That's what it says on the dog shampoo bottle.

We rinsed and repeated three times. Bruno was still malodorous. We rinsed and repeated again. I brushed the shampoo into Bruno's fur with his dog brush. He stood patiently in the shower, waiting to be clean again. He knew it was all his own fault that this was happening.

Finally, after the fourth 'rinse and repeat', Bruno smelled like a Border Terrier again. Wet dog smells better than fox poo, trust me.

High tailed and happy, he stood on a chair whilst I dried him with his hairdryer. Strangely, Bruno likes being dried with the hairdryer. He likes to stand, turning this way and that, in the warm stream of air. He protests when I switch off the hairdryer. When I bath Milly, and dry her with the hairdryer, Bruno pushes her out of the way and nips at my legs to let me know that it's HIS hairdryer. He likes to be dried, even if he isn't wet.

When the gardener comes to tidy up the garden, Bruno follows him round and yips at him, until the gardener gets the message and turns the leaf blower on to Bruno. I usually have to take Bruno back into the house so that the gardener can get on with the task he is here to do. Luckily, he is a dog lover, and Bruno makes him smile.

But – getting back to Fox Poo Friday – here's Bruno, all clean and lovely and sweet smelling … (well, as sweet smelling as a Border Terrier can be). All the excitement has tired him out, so he pads into the middle room, jumps into the old red leather settee, pummels the cushions until he gets them where he wants them to be, and, after turning round and around until he finds the perfect position, he goes to sleep.

I'm quite tired, too. But – no cushions for me – I pad back into the bathroom to clean the last remaining traces of fox poo from the shower. When I've finished that, I need to pad out to the car, clean and disinfect the doggy space in the back, and put the smelly dog bed into the washing machine.

The Adventures of Bruno

Once that's finished, I'll make some camomile tea and sit down for ten minutes and have a rest and read my book.

That's the plan. However, just as I press 'start' on the washing machine, Bruno wakes up, rested and refreshed. He and Milly walk with purpose into the kitchen, both watching me with their heads on one side, waiting expectantly. It's feeding time. And after that it will be time for another walk …

Bruno likes his routine – with just an occasional bit of excitement to add interest to his day …

Bruno Saves the Day (and the Ball)

Have you ever been to Alnmouth? It's near Alnwick, in Northumberland.

There's a beach at Alnmouth, and Bruno does love beaches. Milly likes beaches, too, but not as much as Bruno. The two dogs have very different approaches to the sea. Milly walks delicately over the sand, treading carefully. She avoids piles of seaweed, rockpools and the occasional decomposing seabird. She mostly keeps away from the sea, though she might just dip a furry ladylike toe in the shallowest water. She likes long sandy beaches where the sea is far away and the rocks and rockpools few. She likes to chase her ball where there is no risk of it being thrown inadvertently into a deep pool, or, even worse, the sea itself. Few beaches meet Milly's exacting standards, but she does quite like Alnmouth.

Bruno's approach is quite different, and much more uninhibited. Once released from his lead, he hurls himself down the beach and into the sea at great speed. Then, chest deep in seawater, he stops, and gives a single bark. You can see the realisation dawning that he is almost out of his depth and quite a long way from the shore. There's a moment of stillness – and then he legs it back to the safety of the sand as fast as he can. He covers his embarrassment by chasing any misguided seagulls that happen to have congregated on the beach.

I'm going to tell you about the day that Bruno was a hero. I'm not going to tell you about the time, several years ago now but never to be forgotten, when we went to another of Northumberland's beautiful beaches. It was early morning and nobody was around. There were no Alsatians to be seen, and so I let Bruno off the lead. I thought he'd enjoy a good run.

Actually, I am telling you about it, aren't I? But don't worry. I'll spare you the more distressing details.

The weather had been quite stormy for a day or two, and the beach was strewn with heaps of seaweed, lengths of old blue rope, plastic bottles, bits of wood – all the stuff flung up and abandoned by the retreating tide. Milly found a small, pockmarked rubber ball, and ran round my feet, wanting me to throw it for her. I kept my eye on the ball, but not on Bruno, just for a moment. And a moment is all it takes. He ran ahead, investigating the seaweed, being his curious, beachcombing self.

Out of the corner of my eye I saw something out of place, something that caught my attention. Bruno was rolling over and over in the sand and the seaweed. He'd obviously found something interesting enough that he wanted to wear it.

My heart really did sink. I felt it go. I can't run very well, but I did my best. Bruno was still rolling around. I had a sudden, panicked, thought that perhaps he'd found and eaten something poisonous. Maybe he was rolling around in agony as the poison took effect?

I was already moving down the beach as fast as I could, but I moved a bit faster.

Bruno is still rolling around. But now I can see what he is rolling in. And he seems to be rolling with interest and determination, not in pain.

Do you know the phrase 'mixed feelings'? I had very mixed feelings at that moment. I was relieved and happy that Bruno was safe and well. But I was also horrified at the thought of the task that lay ahead of me on this bright September day.

Bruno, bless him, had found the corpse of a very large, very dead seabird, bigger than a seagull. Bruno obviously found it fascinating, something never before encountered and so obviously requiring dissection and investigation. He was rolling in his find in a spirit of true scientific curiosity.

I'll stop there and let you imagine the rest. I was only sick once.

Are you wondering what Milly was doing whilst all this was happening? Well, she had carried on chasing around the beach with the ancient ball she'd found. She showed no interest at all in Bruno's discoveries. In fact, she seemed to be keeping as far away from Bruno as she could. I rewarded her good behaviour by letting her ride in the front of the car with me on the way back to our holiday cottage. It must have been a relief for her that I didn't make her ride in the back with Smelly Bruno.

Bruno was very quiet for the rest of the day. I think all that scientific research had tired him out, when coupled with the energetic clean-up operation that resulted when we got home. It's a funny thing, but remembering that day has tired me out, too. I think I'll just finish this chapter, and then sit down with a cup of tea. Camomile tea is nice and soothing.

I still haven't told you what happened on the beach at Alnmouth, have I? Bruno was a real 'have-a-go hero' that day, though perhaps a bit careless of his own safety. But it all ended well, with applause and little dog treats for Bruno and relief for Milly. So we'll come back to that day at Alnmouth a bit later on, after I've had my cup of tea.

There's a spirit of anarchy, or lawlessness, about terriers which some people (me, for example) enjoy, and other people find challenging. Maybe there's a reason why the word 'terrier' sounds a bit like terror?

The word 'terrier' comes from the Latin word 'terra', meaning earth, via the Old French 'chien terrier', meaning earth dog. Historically terriers were hunting dogs, and known as earth dogs because of their willingness to follow their prey – rabbits, badgers, foxes – into their burrows in the earth. Terriers like to dig, too, as my garden shows all too clearly.

Bruno's occasional desire to coat himself in what most of us would consider to be noxious substances comes from this same hunting past. By rolling in the corpse of a dead bird or in a great pile of fox poo, the hunter is using the strong smell of these things to mask his own smell. This makes it easier for him to stalk – sneak up on? – his prey. It's an instinct from an ancestral past, even though Bruno's dinner now comes out of a box and the only hunting needed is my trip to the supermarket. The scent-disguising behaviours continue, even though the need for them is long past. I wonder if we humans do anything similar? I don't mean rolling in dead seabirds, but do we ever persist in repeating behaviours which have become redundant and unnecessary?

Bruno and Milly, both terriers, are both clever little dogs in their individual ways. Both understand what I want from them when I give a command and both are generally obedient. They respond to different rewards. Bruno will do much for just one of the tiny bone shaped dog treats I carry in my pocket. Milly is less motivated by food; her reward of choice is a game of 'fetch' with a favourite ball – though any ball will do. Both dogs do that cute and manipulative terrier thing of looking at me with their heads on one side, training me to respond to their appeal. Often, when I give a command, they will look at me in just that way, heads to one side, and I can see their minds at work, the thoughts flying past. 'Should I do what she wants? ' And mostly the answer is 'yes', but just sometimes – and this is what I mean about the anarchy of terriers – they will make a different choice. Bruno usually takes the lead in this. Then they will usually do the opposite of what I wanted them to do, and I swear I can see them laughing. Terrible dog trainer that I am, this makes me laugh, too – though I can see how some people would find it irritating. Maybe terriers are the marmite of the dog world? I like marmite, too.

Bruno's hunting instincts also show themselves in other ways. His favourite game is 'Chase'. He likes me (and Milly) to chase him as he runs away with his toy, or, better still, Milly's toy, or my sock. When I can't keep up with him, he stops and waits for the slowcoach. He also likes to chase pigeons and ducks and squirrels. The pigeons fly away, the ducks swim out on the lake and the squirrels run up trees, but Bruno never gives up hope. He'll chase them again tomorrow.

He is much more cautious and respectful around the big birds, the swans and the geese. Once, long ago, when he was just a young dog, he tried to chase a gaggle of geese. He hadn't realised that geese can be aggressive. They stood their ground, and it ended with them hissing and flapping their wings, chasing Bruno down the field. It's an embarrassing memory. He doesn't like to talk about it.

In spring and summer, when daylight comes early, the dogs and I sit in the conservatory first thing in the morning. I see Bruno, with a look of intense concentration on his face, watching next door's cat as she tootles around my garden, terrorising small birds and mammals. She's quite old and a bit chubby and not as fast as she used to be. I find it wise to wait for her to jump back over the fence before I let Bruno out.

'Better safe than sorry'.

"I need to rehome a small dog. He's a terrier, and tends to bark a lot. Let me know if you're interested. I'll jump over my neighbour's fence and fetch him for you …"

Anon. (Next door's cat??)

Bruno and the Waves

Here we are, back on the beach at Alnmouth. I distracted myself before and told a completely different story, but we're back on track now. Milly likes this beach – plenty of lovely flat sand, and an excellent space in which to chase a ball. Bruno does his usual trick of running into the sea as soon as he is released from the restriction of the lead, finding himself chest deep in seawater and having to doggy paddle, and, after a moment's panic, heading back towards dry land very quickly. He runs up to me enthusiastically, wanting to play, and shakes himself vigorously, sending droplets of seawater all over my trousers. Then he's off again to chase the seagulls, who will keep on flying away.

I throw the ball for Milly and off she goes, grabbing it as it falls and rushing back to drop it at my feet. 'Throw it again! Throw it again!', she yips. And so I throw it again – and again, and again, and again, and again....... Bruno watches the game for a couple of moments and decides he doesn't want to play. He goes back to chasing seagulls. I hear his Lancashire accent again. If I want the ball fetching, I can fetch it myself …

It is rarely a clever idea to try to do two things at the same time. As I'm watching Milly chase her ball, I'm also watching Bruno chasing seagulls, then diving into the sea and rushing out again. I'm distracted from correct ball throwing, not really concentrating on what I'm doing … and a careless or unlucky throw sends the ball flying into the water. Milly does not look happy.

And it is worse than it first seemed. The ball hasn't just gone into the sea. The River Aln joins the sea at Alnmouth (hence the name!) and you can see the river forming what looks like a fast flowing current, initially cutting through the sea at an angle, and the finally merging with it. The ball is bobbing along on that current, being carried away from the shore at some speed. 'Oh dear,' I say to Milly, 'I think I've lost your ball!'

I see a wheaten coloured streak flash past me, there and gone before I can react. 'Bruno!', I yell, 'Come back, now!'. Too late. He's in the water, and in the river current, being carried, like the ball, further away from the shore. I stand, helpless. Is this the end of Bruno? He's quite far away now. Milly and I are helpless, distraught. Well, I'm distraught. Milly, who is a very single-minded little dog, is yipping at me with her 'I want my ball – now!' yip.

I watch, trying desperately to think of something I can do to help, but nothing useful is emerging from the whirling in my head except, repeatedly, 'Is this the end of Bruno?'.

The pink ball is bobbing along still, being carried further and further away. Milly seems to realise the seriousness of the situation and stands aghast at the water's edge. I swear she had a mournful look on her face and tears in her eyes ...

But Bruno is a hero. In the way of 'have-a-go heroes', he has focused on a task, with no thought for his own safety. With a single-minded determination, he doggy paddles as fast as he can, grabs the ball in his teeth, and then – clever Bruno! – turns sideways against the current and swims towards the shore. Within a very few seconds, he can reach the seabed with his feet, and then he pauses for a moment, grips the ball more tightly, and runs out on to the sand. He moves like a wet, hairy bullet towards us, drops the ball at my feet with a 'yip!', and sits down, pleased with himself, expecting a doggy treat – which I give him. And then I give him another. He shakes himself again – I'm quite wet by this time – and goes back to chasing seagulls. Unappreciative of his heroism, they continue to fly away, making seagull squawkings as they go. Despite Milly's protests, I put the ball back into my bag. We've had quite enough excitement with this ball for one day.

How many words can a dog understand? Opinions differ. The psychologist Stanley Coren estimated that the average dog can learn about 165 words, whilst another psychologist, J Paul Scott, put the estimate higher, at 200 words. Whatever the truth of it, I know for certain that Bruno's words include 'lucky' and 'escape'.

Bruno Under Attack

Bruno has not enjoyed a life free from stress and trauma, but terriers are steadfast, courageous little dogs, and Bruno has these qualities in abundance. He faces whatever comes with optimism and resilience.

He has faced illness with patience and, apart from developing an aversion to latex gloves, he has managed to stay friends with our vet, known to Bruno and me as 'Auntie Ruth'. His allergies and skin problems mean that he has to have a weekly bath using his magic medicated shampoo which stops him from being uncomfortably itchy. Into the shower he steps, happy to cooperate for the sake of the little dog treats that I give him once he is in there. I get him good and wet, and then work the magic shampoo into his fur, where the lather must remain for ten minutes in order to do its work. The time passes quite quickly. Once he is all lathered up, I get Bruno to do all his tricks, there on the floor of the shower – 'sit', 'lie down', 'shake paw', 'shake other paw'. Then, 'Bruno, high five!'. We like that one. It can be quite splashy when performed in the shower by a wet dog.

But we save the best until last. This one is Bruno's ace trick. I give him the command 'Lie Down', and then place a doggy treat on the floor beside him, telling him to 'Wait'. And wait he does, until I give the command 'Take It'. Then he takes it very quickly, just in case I change my mind. Despite his streak of anarchy, he never, ever takes the treat until I tell him to take it. Milly can do this trick, too, but she doesn't show Bruno's level of self-discipline. If I ask her to 'Wait' for longer than about 30 seconds, she becomes restless, then grabs the treat with a sidelong look to acknowledge she knows she's failed. She doesn't care.

Bruno is stalwart, though. He waits – and waits. If he thinks I am being too slow in giving the 'Take It' command, he might look at me with appeal in his eyes and whine – but he doesn't move. Perhaps he knows I will reward his patient obedience with a second treat?

And by the time we've done all the tricks three times, the ten minutes are up and we can get on with the business of rinsing Bruno, letting him shake water all over the bathroom – fortunately tiled – and then guiding him towards the hairdryer. I've already told you that he's a strange dog who really enjoys the hairdryer, despite the noise it makes. He's less keen on the smartening up with a hairbrush that comes next, but it is soon over and he tolerates it. Bath time over for another week, Bruno needs a snooze. All this sitting, shaking paws, high fiving and waiting can get tiring for a little dog.

Bruno's skin isn't his only trial in life – he's had problems with his ears, his anal glands and the epulis which grows on his jaw and has had to be surgically removed twice now. It will grow back and may need to be removed again, but thankfully Bruno doesn't know this, so he doesn't worry about it.

He lives in the moment, does Bruno. Like all dogs, he instinctively practises mindfulness. When he's running, he's running, and when he's playing, he's playing – totally focused in the present moment.

He does have a long memory, though, and an awareness of danger. And he knows how to bear a grudge … No 'forgive and forget' for Bruno!

As a puppy and a very young dog, Bruno was a happy, untroubled little soul – sociable and friendly with humans and dogs alike. We used to walk in the grounds of an old manor house, close to where we lived at the time, and Bruno would chase around, off the lead, with his doggy friends – Rosie the Labrador, John the Greyhound and Bonzo the Staffie. It was a golden time.

But nothing lasts for ever, and one day everything changed.

It began like any other day.

We went for one of our longer walks in one of our usual dog-walking places – Bruno, Ba-el (our Doberman, now sadly no longer with us) and me. We were following a path along the edge of a wood, and making our way up hill and down dale round a circular walk that would eventually lead us back to the car park. We had walked this walk many times. It was a lovely day – warm enough to be pleasant, but not so hot that walking became uncomfortable. The sky was blue, the birds were singing and the dogs and I were enjoying ourselves.

All of a sudden, silently and with no warning, a strange dog hurled itself out of the undergrowth to the side of us. It neither growled nor barked, but streaked, like a heat-seeking missile, straight for Bruno, biting and shaking him, seeming intent on causing serious harm. A man, apparently the dog's owner, stood off to the side of the path about 15 yards away, but made no attempt to control or restrain his dog.

Bruno had never met with aggression before, and at first he seemed fixed to the spot, not knowing what to do or how to respond. The other dog, brown and slightly larger than Bruno, ripped Bruno's harness to shreds quickly and efficiently. Once it worked its way past the harness, Bruno's flesh would be an easy target …

Ba-el, our Doberman, seemed paralysed at first, and then retreated behind me, shaking, a continual dribble of urine running fearfully down her leg … She was no help.

There was only me to protect Bruno now. I lifted him up, out of the way, holding him above my head. But the other dog, determined to cause harm, took a great leap and managed to grab Bruno's leg. I had to put Bruno down before serious harm was done as the attacker swung from Bruno's leg. By this time, some instinct had told Bruno what was happening, and he began to try to fight back – but he lacked the other dog's viciousness and ruthlessness. This was something beyond the ordinary, something neither Bruno nor I had ever encountered before.

It's unwise to try and get between two dogs in a dog fight. Chances are you will be hurt. Don't do it.

However, I can give good advice more readily than I can follow it myself. The other dog owner still stood there, still doing nothing. I called out to him for help. He ignored me. I thought Bruno was going to die. Ba-el still stood behind me, still weeing down her leg in panic, still shaking. Who was going to help Bruno if I didn't?

I'm rationalising all this now – I know I would never have forgiven myself if I'd let Bruno come to harm and done nothing to try to prevent it. At the time, though, it was all happening too quickly for clear thought. I raised my walking stick, and whacked the attacker dog, hoping to frighten it off or direct its aggression towards my stick and allow Bruno to escape. The dog seemed impervious to even hard blows, delivered with all the strength I could muster, as if he simply didn't notice them. I looked for his collar, so I could try to restrain him myself – he wasn't wearing one. And still the attack continued. Bruno was tiring now …

In all this confusion, I had been bitten. My hand and arm were soaked in blood – at this stage, I wasn't sure if it was my blood or Bruno's. I held up my bloody arm, and the other dog owner finally moved, albeit slowly. He finally came over and took hold of his dog, with some difficulty. Up to this point, the attacker dog hadn't made a sound, but now he began to growl … His owner produced a choke collar with the lead attached, and slipped the collar over his dog's head. Held in a choke hold, the dog twisted and writhed, but at least was no longer trying to get at Bruno, who had joined Ba-el behind me. He stood shaking and trembling and heavily bloodstained …

'Six of one and half a dozen of the other,' said the other dog owner, almost as aggressive as his dog. 'Both of them were off the lead' – not true. Bruno had been on the lead, though I'd dropped it in the struggle and also in the hope that he might escape.

Before I could say anything, the man ran off, dragging his dog after him. They disappeared into the trees before I had time to move or even think.

I wrapped my hand up in my scarf (I never got the stains out!) to stop the bleeding, and we hurried back to the car and retrieved my mobile phone. I rang for help – someone to drop me off at A&E and take Bruno to our vet. I rang the vet to forewarn her that he was on his way. The nurse at A&E cleaned up my hand, cut off my wedding ring to prevent complications from the inevitable swelling, and gave me some antibiotics. 'That sounds like you met a fighting dog,' she said, 'not just a dog that's a bit nowty'.

I made my way up to the vet's surgery, hand swathed in a dressing. How was Bruno? Things could have been worse, said the vet. He was obviously shaken and very badly bruised, and probably had a strained muscle in his leg – but the blood that had soaked his wheaten fur was mine, not his. His harness had saved him from serious injury. Bruno sat there through this conversation, eating the treats the vet kept feeding him, but far from his usual bouncy little self. 'It's best if you go home,' said the vet, 'and have a quiet evening. Just keep an eye on Bruno and give him something special for tea …'

My friend had rung the police, who came round to my house to inspect the damage to me, Bruno and Bruno's shredded harness. 'That sounds like a dog bred for fighting,' the officer said, 'because dogs will usually bark or growl to give warning before they attack. That silence suggests a fighting dog …' And a dog bred and trained to fight cannot be blamed for doing what the attacker dog had done, particularly when he'd chanced upon a terrier. The ones to blame are the cruel and heartless human beings who choose to find amusement in watching one animal attack another. I wish I'd been able to hit the owner with my walking stick, rather than the dog …

And things changed after that day. We never returned to that walk again, and I became rather more wary of walking in isolated places. Since then we have tended to keep to the places frequented by many dogs and dog walkers. Safety in numbers, perhaps? At least there's someone around to help if need be.

That's not all that changed, though. Bruno, bless him, is still sociable and friendly towards human beings. He does not realise that it is people, rather than other dogs, who are the real threat. He has become, in the words of my book about Border Terriers, 'pro-actively aggressive'. 'Border terriers', my book says, 'are not typically aggressive dogs, though they can't necessarily be trusted if left alone around your neighbour's cat or rabbit. However, Border terriers who encounter aggression from other dogs may become pro-actively aggressive …'

And so it proved with Bruno. Most of the time, he remains friendly towards everyone he meets, human and canine. Occasionally, though, and unpredictably, he may try to attack another dog. Sometimes it is obvious why he might perceive another dog as a potential aggressor – but often it isn't. And Bruno, like me, may have become a tad over-cautious, too, a little lacking in trust … And so poor Bruno can now only be walked on the lead, just in case … His days of running around on the grass with his doggy friends are over forever.

To make matters worse, this was not Bruno's only encounter with aggression. He was once terrorised by two Alsatians, both on the lead, whose owner allowed them to pin Bruno up in a corner, though they couldn't actually reach him … and then very recently, he was attacked again by yet another Alsatian being walked off lead by an owner who had no control over it. Fortunately, no damage was done. A quick-thinking young man, walking close by, ran at the Alsatian, shouting and waving his arms and making himself big – the dog took one look at this scary figure and legged it. Bruno and I laughed. But he still doesn't like Alsatians, or anything that vaguely resembles an Alsatian … though he did make friends with a female Alsatian we used to see on our morning walks. Generally, though, he is 'Alsatianist', and his prejudice, like all prejudice, is born from fear. Sometimes prejudice is based simply on fear and suspicion of anything or anyone that is 'other', different from us. In Bruno's case, his prejudice is born from his experience of aggression. Having met aggression from three Alsatians and one brown Staffie, he now assumes all similar dogs are a threat – despite the evidence of his experience of the many, many non-aggressive, even friendly, Alsatians and brown Staffies he meets. Prejudice isn't rational, though, is it? And so Bruno has to be walked on the lead.

It's a shame. I hope we can overcome his fears eventually. He'd have more fun. And yet the surprising thing, perhaps, is not that Bruno sometimes shows behaviour that is a response to difficult past experience. The surprising thing is that he shows these behaviours quite rarely. Most of the time he is the same friendly little dog he always was – even with Alsatians and brown Staffies.

Like all dogs, Bruno cannot talk about his fears or distress. He can only demonstrate his feelings through his behaviour – a form of communication that can be quite effective. For me, and so for my dogs, the last five years have been filled with sadness and trauma, and that has inevitably affected all of us – but we support each other as best we can. I try to pay attention to my dogs' needs and treat them with consideration, as sentient living creatures. Milly amuses with her playfulness and naughtiness. Bruno comes and leans against my leg and sits quietly with me. And so we move through the days, making the best we can of what remains.

Bruno the Tyrant

When my son was alive, some years ago now, he used to sit with his head on one side, looking at Bruno, also sitting with his head on one side. Then my son would say, 'That dog is a tyrant'.

I used to laugh, and disagree. 'He's not a tyrant,' I'd say, 'he just has very definite ideas about how things should be'. (A bit like my son, really).

But is it possible that my son had a point about Bruno? That Bruno really is a bit of a tyrant?

'TYRANT: a cruel or oppressive ruler. A person exercising power in a cruel, oppressive or arbitrary way' (Oxford English Dictionary)

So perhaps the word 'tyrant' is a bit harsh, a bit of an exaggeration, but Bruno certainly likes to impose his wants and preferences on those around him (i.e. me and Milly) – as witness our ongoing and never-ending battle over the sofa cushions.

'If at first you don't succeed, try, try and try again'. This could be Bruno's motto. He doesn't give up and he doesn't forget. He is nothing if not persistent.

Terriers, like toddlers, exercise 'pester power'. Their aim is identical. If they keep on and on and on and on and on and on and on and on and on and on pestering you, mithering for what they want, eventually you will cave in and give it to them, if only from sheer exhaustion. That's the theory.

However, it is unwise to give in to terrier pester power. What does Bruno learn if I give in? He learns that pester power works. So what is he going to do next time he wants something and I don't immediately give it to him? He's a clever little dog. He knows that it is sensible to use the strategy that was successful last time …

So perhaps you can understand why terrier pester power is best resisted, difficult as that can be? I'd like to say that Bruno never wears me down through his sheer, dogged persistence. I'd like to say that, but I'd be lying. I'm only human. Occasionally, very occasionally, I've slipped – through exhaustion, through necessity or, very infrequently, from amusement. Bruno can make me laugh and he knows as well as I do that if he makes me laugh, I might well reward him with what he wants – or at least with a doggy treat. Dogs are very receptive to human moods and emotions and he knows I like to laugh. So my occasional inconsistencies, infrequent as they are, undermine my attempts at dog training and reinforce Bruno's firm belief that persistence pays off. Because sometimes it does.

So what made my son say that Bruno is a tyrant?

Well, it might have been something to do with the fact that Bruno is much better at training humans than I am at training dogs.

For example:

1. Bruno likes to be taken out for walks, ideally in the countryside or, better still, on a beach. If a walk round the streets where we live is all that is on offer, then he'll take that, though he sometimes shows a bit of glumping disapproval. 'Huh', I can hear him say, 'well, it's not particularly good, is it? But I suppose it's better than nothing …'.

Bruno will not, under any circumstances, poop in our garden. He is very regular in his bowel habits and wants to be taken out, away from our garden, at least once in the morning and once again at teatime. When he was a puppy and a young dog, the territory he defined as 'our garden' gradually became bigger and bigger. On he would trot, obviously anxious to perform his morning ritual, but not until we have walked just a little further … and a little further … and a little further again, until we reached the ideal spot. Which was usually just a little bit further from home than yesterday's ideal spot … Was this Bruno's clever way of extending his walks? Of pushing me to take him for a longer walk than I'd planned? Or am I being over fanciful?

2. Bruno likes to be fed at regular times. He likes his main feed of the day somewhere between 3.30 and 4 pm. On the dot. As the magic hour approaches, he begins to encourage me towards the dog food cupboard, gently at first but then with increasing insistence. I've already mentioned how, if he thinks I am neglecting my dog feeding duties, he will sit down in front of me, head on one side, and yip. And yip. If I still don't move fast enough, he will nudge my leg or nip at my ankle. 'Come on! Move! It's time to feed me!' This can be a little tiresome when I have visitors or am busy with a task, but, as Bruno reminds me, first things have to come first. His 'yip!' can be hard to ignore, rather like a crying baby. Bruno seems to have found an exact tone and pitch to push people (me) into activity. Clever Bruno! Not cruel or unreasonable, but definitely clever.

3. That 'Yip!' can be deployed in all kinds of circumstances. So if Bruno wants to play, he will bring his red fluffy dragon or his green plush sloth, drop it at my feet and yip. If I ignore him, he will pick up the toy, move a few inches in one direction or another, drop it

again – and yip. If I still ignore him, the yip may become a whine and then a single bark. He doesn't give up. He wants me to chase him. So I shout, 'Dragons!' – and Bruno seizes the toy, runs into the conservatory, waits for me to chase him and then runs back again. This chase around the house can go on for quite some time – and it's better still if the weather is fine and the chase can extend into the garden.

I try to define playtime, when it starts and when it ends, but Bruno is having none of it. Anytime can be playtime.

Milly loves to play 'fetch' with her ball – the knobbly purple one is her favourite. Bruno will join in, particularly if I give him a doggy treat when he drops the ball at my feet. But he soon gets bored with this game. I see him look at me with an expression that seems to say, 'If you want the ball that much, you can fetch it yourself'. And back he goes to chasing dragons and weeing on trees. And yipping to remind me to chase dragons with him – he knows I won't wee on trees and doesn't expect it.

4. Every evening, after their meal and their walk, Bruno and Milly like to have a teeth-cleaning chewstick to gnaw on. Sometimes I forget to give these out, or I might be busy cooking my own meal or completing some other task. Once – Oh, dreadful day! – I'd forgotten to replenish our supply of chewsticks. We ran out. I went to get them and there was only the empty packet … Milly didn't much care. Bruno was not happy. The chewsticks need to make their expected appearance within an hour or so of our return from the evening walk or else the 'Yip!' begins …

5. I'm not sure whether this is an example of the kinds of yip-related behaviours which led my son to say that Bruno is a tyrant, but it seems worth mentioning. I wouldn't want to make too much out of this – it's a rare thing – but Bruno has been known to sulk if life is not going quite as he thinks it should. He demonstrates this by the behaviour I've called 'glumping'. His shoulders hunch, his tail goes down, his head goes down and he stomps off on his own and turns his back on the world. It's best to leave him to it – he always comes round eventually, especially if the word 'treats' is mentioned …

A few years ago, my son's ex-girlfriend moved in with us and stayed for about three years. Let's call her Katy. Bruno came to live with us not long after Katy had moved in, and she loved the new puppy and he loved her. And so it continued … but three years later, life changed and Katy moved out. Bruno adapted to her absence, as we do adapt when life changes, and so we went on.

Some five years later, after my son's death, Katy got in contact to offer support, and we have remained in touch. When she first made contact, we speculated about whether Bruno might remember her … we weren't sure. It was agreed that their first meeting in five years would take place by the lake where the dogs and I walk most days. Katy would come with us on our walk and see how Bruno reacted.

Well, Bruno reacted all right. When I opened up the tailgate of the car, he jumped down, and I anticipated that Katy would at least receive the enthusiastic welcome Bruno gives to most people. No such thing. As soon as he saw her, he turned his back, sat down and refused to interact with her at all, even when offered his favourite treats. He glumped. He walked stolidly round the lake, head down, refusing to look at either of us. I could almost hear him saying to Katy, 'You disappear for five years and then expect me to be pleased to see you? Think again. Huh!' Glump, glump, glump.

As we continued round the lake, Bruno gradually relaxed. His body began to look less tense and hunched. He accepted a treat from me – but still ignored Katy. By the time we had almost reached the car again, he was almost ready to at least consider forgiving her – but only if she showed true contrition and gave him lots of treats. She grovelled. By the time we'd arrived back at my house and had lunch, Bruno and Katy were friends again. He's got over it all now and is always pleased to see her. Did he remember her on that first meeting after five years? What do you think?

As I've written all this, I've decided that Bruno isn't really a tyrant. He's a terrier, and a little terrier who likes order, structure and routine. A place for everything and everything in its place. Perhaps these things help him to feel safe? Bruno is a kind and affectionate soul, who tolerates my general fecklessness and lack of organisation very well. He knows that I just need to be reminded, sometimes, about what should be happening and when. It has become Bruno's task in life to be my little furry canine diary. Some people set audible reminders on their phones to help them to structure their day; I have Bruno's gentle but insistent 'yip' to fulfil the same purpose. And his glumpiness tells me when he is finding life difficult.

Sometimes life does get in the way of structures and routines, and we must be flexible, respond to changing circumstances and unexpected events. Bruno recognises these times when they come. He doesn't necessarily like them, but he recognises them. If I am distracted from my duties as Bruno's housekeeper by something frivolous – maybe I want to finish the chapter in the book I'm reading – then Bruno will yip sternly, to remind me of my obligations. If, however, I am distracted by something serious and important, like the washing machine flooding the kitchen, Bruno recognises that this is something that matters. He adopts his 'glumping' stance, and will invariably retire to his memory foam bed by the radiator and wait for the crisis to pass, as it will eventually.

And then he will yip …

Bruno and the Brownies

Be warned. This is quite a sad story, involving a Bruno who ended up feeling very sorry for himself indeed.

We are travelling back in time some ten years. Bruno was not quite two – a teenager in dog years. We lived in a different house then, in a village some ten miles away from our present home. Milly had still not been invented, but we did have another dog – Ba-el, a Doberman. I know I'm going off at a tangent again, but I remember how much Bruno really loved Ba-el. His grief when she died, some seven years ago now, was heart-breaking to see. Eventually, life grew around the grief and he began to enjoy himself again, but it took a while. Even now, years later, if we see a Doberman in the distance Bruno's tail lifts, his ears twitch and he holds himself hopefully – and it brings tears to my eyes to see that hope disappointed as we come closer to the dog and Bruno deflates into the realisation that it isn't Ba-el. Terriers have long memories. Bruno is back, these days, to being high-tailed and happy much more quickly than would happen just after Ba-el died, but he doesn't forget her.

Please don't tell me that Bruno is 'only a dog' and can't feel grief. I might get cross. Perhaps you need to have been friends with a dog yourself before you can fully appreciate that dogs feel emotion in their own way. Trust me, Bruno grieved for Ba-el. I know grief when I see it.

Anyway – back to the brownies! These were not the brownies of folklore – small, hobbit-like creatures of mischief. No. Think chocolate – posh chocolate brownies from a posh chocolate brownie shop; brownies lush and dense with dark chocolate, rich in cocoa solids. In other words, these were brownies posing great peril to little dogs. Perhaps these brownies should have come with a health warning on the label: 'DANGER! Deadly to dogs!' If you are reading this, you are probably a dog-lover, and you will know that chocolate is poisonous to dogs. Too much chocolate isn't good for anyone, but even quite a small amount can kill a dog, especially a small, hairy terrier. Bruno can't read, though, so a warning on the label probably wouldn't have helped.

Don't worry too much. This isn't the last story in this book, so obviously Bruno survived his encounter with posh chocolate, and who knows? Maybe the enjoyment as he ate the brownies repaid his later sufferings.

I blame myself. Maybe I wasn't quite as careful as I could and should have been. I certainly underestimated the level of ingenuity Bruno can show in pursuit of his wants.

This is what happened. At the time, my son and his girlfriend were living in my house. I'd been very busy trying to manage both my job and the sudden admission to hospital of a family member, who had become quite seriously ill. I spent a lot of time in my car, travelling from one place to another, and a lot of time in hospital visiting and all that entails. My son and his girlfriend had had to fend for themselves. Fair enough. They were adults. They'd also had to take on extra responsibility for the dogs and fit that around their own work and college commitments. We were all busy and under pressure of one kind or another.

One Saturday, as I buzzed around in my car, carrying out various necessary tasks, I passed the posh chocolate shop, and noticed an unusual parking space right outside it. A thought floated into my mind and, one illegal U-turn later, I acted upon that thought. From such small, good intentions, unexpected consequences can flow …

Having slid my car neatly into the parking space, I went into the posh chocolate shop and bought six brownies – a small gesture of appreciation, I thought, for the support given by my son and his girlfriend (and I did think they might leave a brownie for me).

When I arrived home, they were out, as I'd known they would be. I left the box of brownies on the kitchen worktop, right by the kettle, with a note saying, 'hope you enjoy eating these xxx'.

Then, after a quick cheese sandwich and energy-boosting coffee, it was time to go back to the hospital …

By the time I'd visited the patient, then gone to the supermarket to replenish our empty cupboards and fridge, and got home, it was after 8 pm as I finally drove into my driveway …

Hmmm. Strange. No sign of my son's car.

I carried my heavy shopping bags into the kitchen. No sign of Bruno. No terrier explosion of greeting. No canine attempts to investigate the shopping bags, no sausage hunt. No tail wagging to greet me. Nothing. Silence. A sense of disturbance in the air. Something has happened here.

My other dog, Ba-el, was on her bed under the breakfast bar in the kitchen, her 'safe place' when she felt challenged by life. She came out only reluctantly, after coaxing and bribery with her own special dog treats. She was very subdued.

I'm worried now. I ring my son's mobile phone, and then his girlfriend's. Both switched off.

I'm even more worried. The house looks just as it normally looks, no sign of disturbance, but it feels wrong. What can have happened here?

And then the house phone rings. It's a stranger, a woman I don't know. Explanations follow. She is a colleague of my son's, an animal-lover and dog owner. He'd rung her for advice – is it true, he'd asked, that chocolate is toxic for dogs?

A picture now begins to emerge. My son's colleague had confirmed that chocolate can, indeed, be dangerous to dogs, and that the higher the content of cocoa solids, the more dangerous it is. She'd told him about the 24-hour veterinary hospital, open on a Saturday evening, that was about 15 miles from our home. She'd given him its telephone number, and now gave it to me.

I'm beginning to understand what has happened here. Bruno, like most terriers, has certain personality traits. He is intelligent, ingenious and persistent, clever at devising strategies to get what he wants. He is also greedy and has a definite sweet tooth, which we don't allow him to indulge. He's not to be trusted around an unattended plate of biscuits left on a low table … I didn't, in that moment, stop to wonder how he'd managed to reach the brownies, high on the kitchen workbench and out of his reach. I just knew he'd done it.

Ba-el was noted for her caution and timidity. She completely lacked Bruno's adventurous spirit and keen curiosity. She liked to play it safe. From puppyhood, she'd always been a very picky eater, refusing most food and dog treats and wanting only her own narrow range of preferred foods. She'd never posed the slightest risk to a plate of biscuits, and usually retreated to her safe place when Bruno was up to no good. She was always well-behaved. And even Ba-el, much bigger than Bruno, could not reach up on to the worktop …

I began to dial the number for the veterinary hospital – and, as I did so, saw my son's car pull into the driveway. In they bounced, he and his girlfriend. They told me how they'd returned home earlier that evening to find Bruno up on the workbench – 'he must have managed to jump up', they said, improbably. Though he hadn't seemed so keen to jump down, even when they walked through the door. They had immediately seen the brownie crumbs, the tell-tale smears around Bruno's mouth and the shreds of white cake box. More importantly, they'd also seen the fortunately intact label showing what had been in the cake box and showing the high cocoa content in the cakes. Bruno had 'scarfed down' all six brownies, and hadn't been sick – though anyone who eats six chocolate brownies deserves to be sick. Don't try this at home.

With great presence of mind, my son had phoned the first person he could think of who would know about first aid for dogs. He'd then followed the advice given and taken Bruno to the veterinary hospital. Whatever needed to happen had happened – you don't need the details. Bruno had not enjoyed it. Then the vet had said that Bruno would be fine, but that she wanted to keep him in overnight for observation. We could collect him the next day after 10 am, but telephone first just in case there was any change.

We settled down for a cup of tea and another cheese sandwich – none of us had had anything to eat. A cake would have been nice at that point …

Just as I reached for the breadknife, the telephone rang. It was late by this time, almost midnight. Who on earth could be ringing at this hour? It was a worrying moment. We had a family member in one hospital ten miles away, and our dog in another hospital 15 miles in the opposite direction. It was unlikely that a ringing phone so late at night was bringing good news …

But do you remember that I said that Bruno is persistent and good at getting what he wants?

It was the receptionist from the veterinary hospital who was phoning us. 'Can you come and get your dog?', she said, 'now, please?' Bruno had begun to whine, howl and bark as soon as my son and his girlfriend had left the building. He couldn't see them, but he had seemed to know the exact second they went through the door.

Now, some two hours later, Bruno was still whining, howling and barking. Incessantly. He had refused to be consoled or bribed and was disturbing the other sick animals (not to mention the staff). The vet had said that keeping him overnight had been a 'belt and braces' precaution, but that it would obviously now be best for everyone if he just went home immediately.

It was 1 am as we arrived back at the veterinary hospital. As soon as we opened the car door, we could hear Bruno's unmistakeable terrier bark, loud, persistent and continuous. He was incredibly pleased to see us and was no longer subdued by his adventure. He wasn't pleased that we'd left him in this alien place of strange smells, unfamiliar people and poorly animals – but he'd forgive us if we took him home – now. So we did.

CODA:

I haven't explained how Bruno managed to steal the brownies in the first place, have I? How had he managed to get up onto the workbench, surely too high up for a little dog to jump? It was a mystery, and it remained a mystery.

But then, one Sunday a few weeks later, Bruno was busted. The mystery was solved. I'd like to say that this was down to my Miss-Marple-like skills in detection, but it wasn't. It was pure chance.

I'd cooked a leg of lamb, which lay resting on the workbench, well out of reach of the dogs.

Then I'd gone upstairs for a few minutes, leaving the kitchen unattended. Bruno must have been too focused on what he was doing to hear me returning, and, as I re-entered the kitchen, there he was, in the act of preparing to help himself to a lamb dinner ... I think the police call it 'going equipped'.

There was an old table in the middle of the kitchen where we used to eat if we couldn't be bothered to carry food through to the dining room. Around the table were four old heavy wooden chairs – I still have them in my kitchen now. Each chair had a cushion on it, secured by ties fastened round the back of the chair. And there was Bruno, cushion ties between his teeth, pulling one of the chairs over towards the workbench ... Soon he would have got it close enough that he could use it as a jumping off point to get up to the lamb, resting fragrantly on its plate ... so tempting. Bruno loves lamb.

He looked at me. I looked at him. Tail down, he retreated into the dining room. He knows when he is beaten. The chair cushions went in a bin bag and then up in the loft ... And that was the end of Bruno's career as a cat burglar (though I did, after lunch, give him some of the lamb).

Bruno's Big Adventure

Adventures aren't always fun or funny, even after they are over. Sometimes they are just downright difficult or scary. A few months before we all entered the Land of Lockdown, Bruno had an adventure which seemed, at the time, like it might be his last.

It started one Tuesday in the dark, wet days of late October, 2019. Bruno had a tummy upset – I'll spare you the details. Both ends. Milly hid under my chair. She's a bit squeamish sometimes, and underneath a chair probably seemed like the best place to be. In fact, I'd have liked to hide under the chair myself, but I'm too big. I wouldn't fit.

In a pause when Bruno was asleep, I rang our vet. 'Bring him up,' she said – so we set off in the car. It's always a bit of an adventure taking Bruno to see the vet. There's a point in the journey when we turn round a corner and he realises where we are going. And then he starts. 'Yip! Bark! Howl! Yip! Yip! Yip!' He's not happy. We go to the back door of the surgery now so that he doesn't have to face the trauma of the waiting room – though I think that maybe he's just trying to avoid the weighing scales since he's a little – how can I say this tactfully? – a little on the round side.

He was quite subdued this time, though, and made no protest when the vet opened the back door and took us through to the treatment room. That told me that he must be feeling poorly … But he'd stopped being sick by this time, and things had calmed down a little bit at the other end. The vet wasn't too worried. I wasn't too worried. Bruno was just relieved to get out of the surgery quite quickly. The vet's parting words were, 'Bruno has probably just picked up a bug. It should be out of his system in a couple of days, but it's quite likely that Milly will catch it, too' … The image of two vomiting dogs with diarrhoea came into my mind … Let's focus on the positives. Thank God I have tiled floors …

We went home with some medication and instructions about a light diet – only plain rice and a very small amount of chicken. This isn't Bruno's favourite diet, but – tough. The vet had said he should have a light diet, so that was what he was going to get. We made it back home without incident. I even stopped off at the supermarket for more chicken. Bruno slept through the whole journey, and, after a sniff round the living room when we arrived home, he went back to sleep on his dog bed. I think he'd noticed the overwhelming smell of disinfectant which permeated my whole house …

A couple of days passed. Bruno seemed to be improving slowly. There was no more vomit, and the poo was less copious and more infrequent (and, if you really want to know, more solid). He ate the chicken and rice (small amounts only) with an air of a dog whose patience was being sorely tried – but he ate it. He took the medication with a good grace and only a little bribery. Milly seemed fine – her usual feisty little self. Perhaps, I thought, we've escaped the worst.

My mother would have called that thought 'tempting providence' – and so it proved.

On Friday morning, at 5 am, I was awakened by an agitated Milly, obviously desperate to get out into the garden. She'd been sick on the floor – 'Thank God the floor's tiled,' I thought again. And 'Oh dear. Oh dear,' I said to myself.

It was a wild, dark night in early November, and the rain was falling relentlessly. It was the kind of rain that leaves you soaked and frozen in seconds. As I opened the back door, Milly shot through it like a little hairy bullet and disappeared under the trees to do what she needed to do. It took a while …

Finally, she appeared back on the path, dripping wet, cold and looking deeply sorry for herself. The vet had given me the medication she'd need if – when – she caught Bruno's bug, and she took it very readily, as if she knew it would make her feel better. I dried her off, and she settled herself back on her dog bed and went to sleep. I'd have quite liked to go back to sleep myself, but there was still the doggy vomit on the floor, waiting to be mopped up …

And where was Bruno whilst all this was happening? He was still on his dog bed, facing away from me – apparently sleeping, undisturbed by all the commotion. That wasn't like Bruno, who's normally such a nosy, curious dog, wanting to join in with whatever might be happening. 'Perhaps he's tired after his days of unwellness,' I thought. I was tired after his days of unwellness, so it seemed reasonable that he might be even more tired.

I decided to harden my heart and wake him up – it was almost 6 am by now. 'I can take him out for his first wee of the day,' I thought, 'and then maybe we can all go back to sleep for a while.'

Do you know that poem about the best laid plans of mice and men ganging oft agley? It's by Robert Burns. I'm not sure what 'agley' means, but it doesn't sound good, does it?

'Bruno, come on,' I called – no response. I rattled the treats bag – that always gets Bruno moving. No response. I went over to the dog bed. Bruno was lying on his side, not asleep as I'd thought, but with his eyes wide open and looking around anxiously. He looked frightened. I stroked him – 'Come on, Broons,' I said, 'Let's go for a wee.' He looked at me and whimpered softly for a second or two – but he didn't move.

Bruno is quite a big dog for a Border Terrier, and is quite heavy, but I picked him up as best I could and tried to set him on his feet. He just fell over onto his side. He couldn't stand or even move. I tried again. The same thing happened. Bruno whimpered. Inside my head, I whimpered, too.

I settled him into a more comfy-looking position, and gave him one of his favourite treats, which he sniffed, but didn't eat. Time to ring the vet.

So I rang the out of hours veterinary hospital for advice. 'Bring him in,' they said.

It was still dark, still cold, still raining hard. Bruno couldn't walk out to my car, at the far end of the garden. I opened the car door and made a bed on the back seat for Bruno, and then I carried him out and made him as comfortable as I could in the back of the car. It isn't the easiest thing in the world to do, to carry 12.5 kilos of limp Border Terrier all the way down the path whilst walking with a stick – but we made it. Eventually.

Bruno lay, immobile and unresisting, as I strapped him in, his eyes big and wide and glistening in the darkness. He whimpered softly as I closed the car door …

I went back to the house to check on Milly and lock the doors. Poor little Milly, still asleep, would have to be abandoned to manage as best she could whilst Bruno and I went to doggy A&E. I put out clean water for her and left her to it. Poor Milly.

Whilst I was obviously in a better state than Bruno, I don't think

I was at my usual peak of efficiency. Despite having been to the veterinary hospital several times before – remember the brownies? – I got lost. The satnav told me slowly and patiently which way to go – but I still got lost.

But we made it in the end, and I pulled into the car park with a strong sense of relief. The receptionist came out and carried Bruno through to the doggy triage area. 'Please take a seat in the waiting area,' she said, 'and someone will be out to speak to you as soon as possible.'

So I sat in the waiting area and I waited. I chatted to a man with a little French Bulldog who had begun to give birth to puppies but then developed complications. She lay there in her basket, patiently. And then they went through to see the vet and we chatted no more. I waited. A woman came out from the treatment area with a Border Collie with a bandaged leg. 'We're just waiting for some antibiotics,' she said. We chatted. The antibiotics arrived. They left. I waited. I waited some more. Time passed as it always does, but it passed quite slowly.

Finally, a woman came out of the treatment area, this time looking for me. 'I've examined Bruno,' she said, 'and we're not really sure what's wrong. We've managed to get him to stand, with some difficulty, but he can weight bear. His right side is actually OK, but he seems to have developed a weakness all down his left side. That could be due to a number of things ...'

So what was the plan? Well, she was going to bring Bruno out to the waiting area to sit with me, because she thought he'd be happier with me than in a cage in the treatment room. They wanted to keep an eye on him for the next hour or so in the hope he would continue to improve slowly. It was after 7 am by this time, so they suggested

Annie Jones & Emily Grundy

I stay at doggy A&E until 8 am, and then make my way with Bruno to our own vet, who would open at 8.30. They'd phone ahead to let the vet know we were coming.

Bruno walked out of the treatment area with the veterinary nurse. He was terribly slow and very wobbly, and had to keep stopping to centre himself and get his balance – but he was able to stand and able to walk (sort of). Things could have been worse. I'd thought he might be about to embark on his final big adventure …

We waited in the waiting area, Bruno and me. We had a tiny walk to the water bowl and another tiny walk so he could say hello to a passing Yorkshire Terrier. 8 am arrived, and by now Bruno was a little less wobbly. I went to bring my car right up to the door of the doggy A&E, and the receptionist walked Bruno out to me and lifted him back into his bed on the back seat.

Bruno lay there, big eyes watching me, wondering what was happening. I was wondering what was happening, too. 'It's a bit of a mystery', the veterinary nurse had said, and so it was, and so it remained. It would take too long to go into great detail about the next few months of Bruno's life, so I'll just give you the short version.

After leaving doggy A&E, we drove the 12 miles or so to our own vet. Bruno's Auntie Ruth was not at work that day, so he made the acquaintance of Emily, another vet. It was fine. They seemed to understand each other.

Bruno stayed at the vet's surgery all day, and had various tests to try to work out what was wrong. I hoped for the best. I left Bruno with his new Auntie Emily and went home to check on Poor Milly – remember her? Abandoned to her fate some hours earlier?

She was INCREDIBLY pleased to see me. She'd been sick again

– there were two more piles of doggy vomit on the tiles – and once again shot out of sight and under the trees when the door was opened. Once again she was gone for a while, and came back looking visibly relieved and with her tail wagging. I gave her more medication and some chicken and rice. No problem getting Milly to eat chicken and rice. She almost ate the plate, too. 'I have to feed you little and often, Milly,' I told her. She did not look impressed. She went and sat by the fridge and looked hopeful, but soon realised that her hope was not going to be realised. The fridge door stayed shut. Milly took her ball – always her comfort object – and went back to her basket and back to sleep …

The day passed, as days do. The vet phoned a couple of times to update me. Over the day, Bruno's left-sided weakness had improved slowly, as had his walking, though he remained a bit hesitant and unsteady, and seemed to struggle just a little bit to walk in a straight line. No vomiting. No diarrhoea.

Apart from showing that Bruno had a tummy bug (we knew that!), all the test results were clear. They were keeping an eye on him. Finally, around 4.30 pm, I got the call to go and collect him, along with more medication and instructions on diet and exercise (not much food and short lead walks only).

Days passed. More follow up appointments with the vet, more mystery. Bruno continued to make slow progress. His diarrhoea took a while to clear completely, and we had a fun day on New Year's Day collecting poo samples, so the vet could check that the infection had finally resolved (it had – the samples were clear).

The exact cause of his collapse into immobility remains a mystery. It might be some kind of neurological problem or hereditary weakness or something to do with getting old or something else entirely. Bruno continued to improve, though, and by mid-January all trace of weakness seemed to have vanished. He was walking and even running quite normally. He runs about less frequently than he used to do, but, after all, he is getting older now. So am I and I run about less frequently than I used to do, too. He seems happy enough.

After long discussions with Ruth and Emily, the vets and I decided that there was no point in further, intrusive tests at this stage, particularly since Bruno gets so distressed when I abandon him (as he sees it) with the vet. His test results had shown no need for any further investigations, so it seemed best to let him get on with his doggy life for whatever time is left to him. On veterinary advice we changed to a gluten-free diet – fortunately, he likes it – and I continue to monitor him for more 'funny turns'. So far, so good. As I write this five months later, Bruno has not had any more funny turns and is getting on with his doggy life in Lockdown Land.

'To die will be an awfully big adventure', says J M Barrie's Peter Pan – and for a time, back in November and December, I thought Bruno was on the edge of this awfully big adventure. This wasn't a stupid thing to think. Bruno's favourite sister and litter mate, Ruby, had a very similar 'funny turn' in December, just before their eleventh birthday, but, sadly, Ruby did not improve and died later that same day.

So Bruno was lucky. He was always the biggest and strongest of the puppies when they were all still with their mother, and maybe that helped him now. Life goes on for him and he continues to have his everyday adventures and he seems to enjoy life, even in Lockdown Land. Long may that continue!

The Adventures of Bruno

Are you wondering what happened to Milly? Well, she's fine. Her tummy bug cleared up within 24 hours. She was starving and demanding FOOD by the following day. There was no more doggy vomit and her other end subsided into ordinariness equally quickly. She had no mysterious symptoms and no need for further veterinary intervention. She did have a little adventure of her own when she hurt her paw in February, but that was soon dealt with and she's fine now.

Bruno has just brought his ball into the dining room where I am sitting as I type this. He dropped the ball on my foot and looked at me in hope and expectation. 'The garden? Throw the ball? Dog treats if I fetch it?' Sometimes he communicates his wants very clearly. So it's time to go! Where did I leave the dog treats, I wonder??

Bruno — What Next?

Bruno and I are growing old together. Both of us are closer to our end than we are to our beginning. But we are not quite done yet – maybe we have time for a few more adventures before we disappear into silence?

Bruno is now a little grey around the muzzle and gets tired more quickly than he used to do. I bought the memory foam dog bed, 'for dogs who are getting on in years', and Bruno immediately claimed ownership of it – though he allows Milly to use it sometimes. Bruno sleeps in it most nights, and, after all, Milly is that bit younger. But maybe it's only fair to buy her a memory foam bed too? It's good to be **prepared**.

Bruno and I agree that every day can be a new adventure. Every day brings with it the possibility of something exciting, or surprising, or interesting, or amusing or challenging. Neither of us can know what tomorrow will bring – visitors? Something special to eat. A trip to a beach? Or maybe it will bring nothing in particular – just the comfort of ordinariness and familiarity.

Today is the first day of spring, a time of new beginnings. Bruno and Milly have both been quite excitable and 'barky' all day – maybe they sense a new energy in the air as the darkness and coldness of winter recede. They greeted old friends and made a new one as we walked round the lake this morning. Dogs and owners all seemed energised by the sunshine – everyone was friendly, chatty and cheerful. Bruno was high tailed and happy, interested anew in all the smells and sights, keen to wee on as many trees and bushes as he could manage. It was a good walk.

So we carry on, day by day by day. We don't know what is next, but we are ready for whatever comes. We are looking forward to new adventures – though I really do hope that they won't involve fox poo or dead seabirds.

The End?

ONE DAY
LIFE
CHANGED ...

Bruno in Lockdown Land

At the end of Bruno's last adventure, we were toddling off together into a quiet old age. Bruno was enjoying walks round the lake, and the more exciting walks he had with April, our new dog walker. We were looking forward to going back to Northumberland for more walks on the lovely beaches. Bruno might have had a secret hope that he'd find some more long dead sea birds to roll in, but we won't talk about that. Life was fairly quiet, and predictable in lots of ways, but Bruno enjoyed trips out in the car (as long as we didn't head to the vet's) and he liked exploring new places … He was quite waggy tailed and curious about life.

None of us knows what the future will bring, though, do we? Life is full of surprises and some of them are not always much fun, whether for people or for dogs.

One day, quite suddenly it seemed, life changed. April the Dog Walker appeared no more. Bruno waited by the door for her every Monday morning, but she didn't come. And then she didn't come on Wednesdays, either. And – even worse – the ordinary walks with me changed, too. No more walks round the lake. No more trips in the car to lovely places with lots of new scents to follow. Walks began to follow a pattern Bruno disapproved of. On would go his harness, then Milly's, and then we all walk out of the gate – where are we going? Might it be a field or a beach or a forest?

But no. We walk round the block or round the streets nearby. There's the odd tree to wee on, and a lot of walls and gateposts to investigate. Milly gets excited when she sees a cat under a parked car or sitting on a wall – 'Grr, snarl, let me at it …! Bark, bark!'. Bruno looks at her with bemusement – hasn't she learned that cats have claws? He doesn't join in.

Bruno doesn't approve of all this change and he is exceptionally good at signalling his disapproval. He glumps. He is incredibly good at glumping. Have I told you before about Bruno's glumping? I may have done – I don't remember – but it's worth describing again now because we are seeing so much more of it.

When Bruno disapproves of something, his head sinks down between his shoulders and he hunches himself up. His tail goes down and remains unwagged. He refuses to look at me and refuses even favourite treats – until the temptation becomes too great, and then he'll snatch the treat, and turn his back on me to eat it. And continue to glump. Sometimes, when we have our daily walk around the streets, his glumpiness is such that he just pads round without looking to left nor right or sniffing anything. He heads around the block with stoic patience and glumps back into the garden at the end of the walk. When he is in this mood, the only thing that bounces him out of it is if we see the elderly lady who walks three – three! – Alsatians. I try to avoid her by walking at times when she's unlikely to be about – but she's not always predictable and she's taken me by surprise on more than one occasion.

As you know, Bruno does not like Alsatians. He lumps them all together into the category of 'dogs I don't like'. He is what our vet has called 'breedist' and 'Alsatianist'. Twice he has had unpleasant encounters with thuggish Alsatians who tried to bite him – so now he assumes all Alsatians are thugs and criminals. Of course this isn't true – Alsatians can be lovely dogs, I tell him – but Bruno is having none of that namby-pamby stuff. As soon as he sees an Alsatian, his hair stands up, he makes himself as big as he can and he lunges forwards, barking with all his might. He won't be intimidated! He'll show those Alsatians who is boss! I'll leave you to imagine what happens when we go round a corner, and there, 20 yards away, are THREE Alsatians. Luckily, the Alsatians are well bred and they ignore him, walking past with their noses in the air, laughing at the common barker ... This just annoys Bruno even more. These encounters, thankfully, have happened only rarely. They do pull Bruno out of his glumpiness, but I think I prefer glumpiness. It's easier to deal with.

Time passes, though, and we get used to a changed reality, adjust to a 'new normal'. That's true for dogs as well as for people.

I've watched, and learned the Alsatian lady's schedule and we mostly manage to avoid her or to see her (and her dogs) only in the far distance. Bruno might growl a bit, but he knows, deep down, that it's wise to keep a low profile when the Alsatians haven't seen him. He's learned that even in Lockdown Land there are interesting walls to see and smells to sniff. He no longer pauses as we pass my car, waiting for me to open the door, and he no longer goes to wait for April the Dog Walker. He knows, now, that she isn't coming.

He's noticed, too, that we no longer have visitors and we haven't been to any beaches in a long time. Bruno isn't quite sure what's happening – how do you explain a pandemic to a dog? But he knows that life has changed, and he's not at all sure that he approves of most of the changes. Change is unsettling for Bruno and he misses his old routines. He even misses visitors, much as he used to complain when he felt they'd stayed too long! He quite likes the fact that I'm always at home – he knows there's an upside for every downside –

and I suppose that he's adjusted to the new reality without too much difficulty. Milly, as usual, has just quietly got on with life, taking each day as it comes, happy enough as long as I remember to throw her ball around the garden for her … But Bruno finds it all a bit confusing and, sometimes, unsettling …

Cross Bruno

But – things could be worse. It's taken Bruno some time to understand this, but he's getting there now. Milly might not be his ideal doggy companion, but she's better than nothing. He enjoys being out in the garden, barking at passers-by – especially if they happen to be canine passers-by. He particularly enjoys barking at the American bulldog who lives up the road – he hurls defiance from behind the safety of our high, locked gate. It's all good fun. The American bulldog gets told off if he barks back, and that's even more fun. Bruno is finding new interests in life …

He's come to understand that things could be much worse. I remembered to buy lots of dog treats before we went to live in Lockdown land, so we aren't going to run out. Bruno is reassured by the sight of the dog food stacked in the pantry. Bruno misses the old man we used to see when we walked round the lake – the one who always had a pocket full of little fish-shaped dog biscuits. Bruno liked him – and the biscuits. But no doubt we'll all be back there again eventually, when life changes again.

And in the meantime, Bruno has me and Milly for company. He has enough to eat and a safe supply of treats. He has his very own trees in the garden and can practise precision weeing whenever he likes. And he knows that, with a bit of yippy persuasion, I'll go outside and throw a ball for Milly and a rubber chewing stick for him. There's no fox poo in the garden, and there are no decomposing sea birds – but nothing can be perfect, after all.

Things could definitely be worse, he reflects. Bruno takes a moment to feel sorry for all the unlucky dogs who don't have other dogs for company or gardens to play in. He feels especially sorry for the very unlucky dogs who don't have their own trees. He knows he's lucky, as things go in Lockdown Land.

So his shoulders relax, his head comes up, his tail resumes its usual wagginess and he will look at me again, glumpiness forgotten. Time for another walk around the block …

Annie Jones & Emily Grundy

Bruno and Milly – plotting?

Bruno Breaks the Rules (but not the cup)

Bruno, like most terriers, isn't really a fan of mindless obedience. If I tell him to do something, ('Sit', 'Walk', 'Sshh', 'Fetch' etc.), he normally seems to understand what it is that I want him to do – and then he makes a choice about whether or not to do it. Probably 90 to 95 per cent of the time he will do as I ask, but he sits there, head on one side, and CHOOSES. 'Shall I sit? Why not? – Keep her happy. There might be a treat in it …'

Sometimes his natural contrariness gets the better of him and he becomes deaf. Perhaps he simply doesn't feel like sitting right now – so he won't. He'll do it in his own time, when he's good and ready, and not just because I say so …

Sometimes the red mist descends and then he simply MUST follow that scent, chase that squirrel, bark at that Alsatian, whatever I say.

Sometimes, though, it's his innate curiosity that gets the better of him. Terriers are seekers and searchers. They like to know what's going on – check it out, sniff it, wee on it if necessary. Sometimes this innate curiosity can lead to rule breaking. And, of course, the more rules there are, the easier is becomes to break one. And once you've broken one rule, it's easier to break the second …

There are a lot of rules in Lockdown Land, and many of them are new and unfamiliar. That's difficult for everyone right now, and Bruno, like a lot of us, can struggle at times. He's a clever little dog – but he does have his limitations. I've shown him a picture of the coronavirus, explained to him (as best I could), what it is and what it can do – but he's never seemed to be taking in my explanations. He sniffed the picture without much interest ('Nothing to eat here. Move along'). Then he yawned, farted, pushed Milly off the dog bed and went to sleep. Perhaps I don't speak Terrier well enough to be able to explain things properly?

Social distancing, for example – I don't think Bruno has got his head round that at all. He doesn't like all dogs, but he does like some. When we go out for a walk, Bruno likes to greet the dogs he regards as friends – and there's not much social distancing in anal gland sniffing. He likes to greet their owners, too – especially the ones who carry dog treats in their pockets. He looks at them with appeal in his eyes, and tells them quite clearly, 'She starves me, you know …' – and it works every time.

Except that now it doesn't. Life in Lockdown Land, with its shielding, self-isolating and social distancing, means that we meet fewer dogs and fewer owners than we used to do. Even if we do meet a dog and a treat-carrying owner, we humans, obedient to the rules as we are, tend to greet each other from opposite sides of the street and maintain the proper social distance. We keep our dogs close by us – no fraternising! And so there's no saying hello to doggy friends close up and personal, and there's no free treats from those owners who have the perceptiveness to see beyond Bruno's well-fed (even chubby) exterior to the starving dog beneath.

Yet again Bruno's life has changed in ways that don't entirely meet with his approval. And maybe I've been a bit unclear about the rules, too. Under Lockdown, we were supposed to go out once a day only, and do everything needful in that one trip. Well, we only need to go out for Bruno's walks – and, as he still refuses to poop in the garden, we really need to go out twice – two walks a day. I keep them brief – no more than half an hour each – but maybe I am giving mixed messages – We must stick to the rules (except that one) …

I've told you before that Milly and Bruno like car rides. Usually, when we all get in the car, we're going somewhere they will enjoy (except when we are going to see the vet, but we don't do that too often).

Our move to Lockdown Land has meant that the car is resting, undriven and unused, in its parking place in the garden. No trips out. No exciting walks in new places, or even in the old places we used to drive to. Bruno has only been in the car once in – weeks and weeks! He's lost count how many weeks. 'It's not fair,' he thinks, 'she never even opens the car door.' Glump. Glump. Glump.

When I look at Bruno in this mood, I remember a story told to me recently by one of my nieces. Her little girl, Clemmie, is nearly three. One day, Clemmie figured out how to unlock the garden gate … Like Bruno, Clemmie has her doubts about Lockdown Land. Down the street she ran, shouting, 'I WANT TO SEE PEOPLE!' I think Bruno might like to run down the street shouting, too – 'I WANT PROPER WALKS, AND PEOPLE WITH TREATS, AND CAR RIDES!'

I did tell you, didn't I, that Bruno enjoys car rides?

Well, a few days ago we went for our usual early evening stroll around the estate where we live. It had been a very warm day. I was tired, and perhaps a little less observant than usual? There was nobody around, the streets seemed deserted, and so I let Bruno's extending lead extend a little further than I'd normally allow – 'Give him a bit of freedom,' I thought, 'Let him have a sniff round …'. Milly was with us, but she tends to leave her explorer outfit at home and sticks close by my legs.

I relaxed my guard. Was this foolish? Probably.

As we ambled along in the sunshine, I saw a big van parked by the side of the road. It's often parked there, close by the owner's house. He's a builder, so his van is full of tools and boxes and things that builders need, I guess.

On we ambled, and, just as we drew level with the van, the sliding door along the side nearest to us flew open, and out jumped the owner, his hands full of something or other. I don't know who was more surprised. He hadn't been able to see us coming and we didn't know he was in the van. Social distancing went out of the window – we were probably about 6 inches apart, rather than 6 feet.

There was a moment of confusion as the owner – let's call him Mr Swann – tried to jump back into the van and I tried to move back the way we'd come. It was only a moment, but it was all the time that Bruno needed to take advantage of the situation – don't forget I'd allowed him a longer lead than usual. Silly me.

Into the van he leapt, before I could stop him. OK, he might have been thinking, it's not a car, but it's better than nothing … For an elderly dog, he moved pretty quickly …

I tried to pull Bruno back and Mr Swann tried to avoid getting tangled up in the dog lead. Things got dropped or knocked over as Bruno tried to elbow Mr Swann out of the way and pull Milly and me into the van with him … Somewhere, on top of one of the boxes, there must have been a cup of (fortunately cold) coffee. As Bruno careered into the boxes, the cup fell. It bounced. The coffee flew everywhere. Why is it that a fairly small amount of liquid can cover such a large area? Have you ever dropped a pint of milk and seen how much mess can follow? Well, the inside of Mr Swann's van looked pretty wet. It smelled of cold, milky coffee.

Milly, smug in her good behaviour, retreated behind me. She understands social distancing.

Chaos and confusion reigned for a few seconds as Bruno dashed about inside the van. Fortunately, Mr Swann is a dog lover, and even more fortunately, he has a sense of humour.

Between us, we got Bruno out of the van and back onto the pavement. He wasn't happy – hadn't we understood that he wanted to go for an outing? He looked at Mr Swann, and then at me, and then back at Mr Swann and back at me. We were impervious to all pleas. I'd shortened Bruno's lead and moved back along the pavement to the appropriate 6 feet away. Mr Swann jumped out of his van (again) and closed the door firmly. And then he locked it. He said goodnight, still laughing, and went into his house.

Bruno got the message – no outings for him. He glumped all the way back to our house.

Since that evening last week I've kept him on a short lead as we go for our Lockdown Land walks around the estate. If I see that Mr Swann's van is parked by the roadside, we walk along the opposite pavement – just in case. Bruno always slows down and looks at the van with hope in his eyes – just in case … We keep walking.

But despite his disappointments and his glumpiness, Bruno is generally an optimistic little soul. He doesn't give up. Maybe one day there will be car rides again?

Milly the Oppressor
By Emily

Lockdown has been taking a toll on Milly and, (unlike Bruno) she has been turning into a menace. She has now destroyed 27 pillows. Even though most of the pillows are double the size of her. When she is angry, she gets an adrenaline rush and turns into a … CANINE SHREDDER!!!

Bruno is enjoying quarantine because now he is older, he likes do things with as little effort as possible (this includes protecting his pack). OK let me explain … When a dog has more than one owner the people that live with them are seen as in that dog's pack. Dogs believe they must protect their pack from all danger. Now Milly and Annie are always staying inside and Annie never goes out without the dogs, this makes Bruno's job mega easy.

Lockdown has some disadvantages too (as you would know if you read The adventures of Bruno 12) like: NO long walks, the gardener not visiting to tidy the garden, no friends like Emily and Rachel can visit and NO rolling in strange new scents at the beach or park.

Annie and the dogs are finding new ways to entertain themselves in quarantine and they have each found a new activity they enjoy. Annie found the joy of singing in an online choir. Bruno has found the pleasure of stealing leftover chamomile tea and getting a fuzzy tummy and Milly has learnt a better way to rearrange pillows.

When you look at Milly and Bruno you can imagine what they would look like if they were human. Milly would look like a chubby version of Ariana Grande on a bad hair day and Bruno would look like Paul Hollywood but with a brown Santa Claus beard.

But after all the experiences they have had, the Government might loosen the ropes in a few weeks and then Milly and Bruno can revisit the lake and the beach and see April the lovely dog walker.

Oppressor is a strong word but the way Milly demolishes the poor settee cushions suggests it is fitting.

Milly the Canine Shredder with Bruno's toys … he was asleep, so she seized her chance to take the dragon!

Bruno and the Cone of Shame

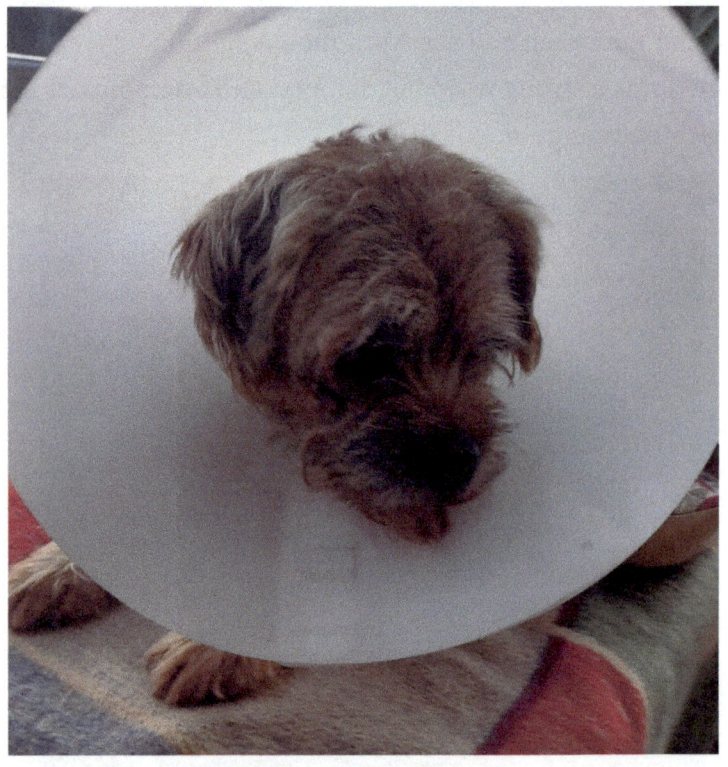

Aging brings indignities, as you will learn if you live long enough – as I hope you do. As you grow older, you find that your body struggles to do things it used to do quite easily, like climbing stairs, but insists on doing things you'd really prefer it didn't do, like putting your bladder into overdrive or nodding off five minutes before the end of your favourite TV programme. Aging brings indignities for people, but it brings indignities for dogs, too. There are also compensations, of course. As we get older, we worry less about what other people think of us, for example – but at the moment, Bruno is much more focused on the indignities of aging rather than the compensations.

One of the indignities Bruno has faced in the last couple of years, as he enters into doggy old age, is a tendency to develop warts, or skin tags on various parts of his body. For the most part, these just sit there doing no harm to anyone, and simply mean that the groomer has to be careful when giving him a haircut and I have to be careful when combing him with the Furminator (isn't that a wonderful name?).

Impermanence is part of all life, though. Nothing stays the same and everything changes. During the Lockdown Summer, one of the things that changed for Bruno is that a wart appeared on the right side of his face, just beside his eye. At first, it just sat there, like the other warts, minding its own business – but then it began to grow. 'Hm,' said the vet, 'I think it's just a wart, but if it gets any bigger, it will need to come off …'

It got bigger – and bigger. When Bruno scratched his ear, his paw would catch the wart and make it bleed. As it healed, it would itch, as healing wounds do, so Bruno would scratch it again, on purpose this time. And of course, that would make it bleed again … and so the cycle continued. Dogs can have mucky paws, since they don't wear shoes – even dogs who have to have a bath once a week with magic shampoo, as Bruno does. These mucky paws can spread infection, especially if they come into contact with an open wound, like the one on Bruno's face when he scratched the wart. If the wound becomes infected, that can be serious, even life-threatening – and so in consultation with Vet Emily and Vet Zoe, I decided that the time had come to book Bruno in for a little operation. Wart removal. Not a big deal. 'And', I told myself and Bruno, 'once the wart is removed,

Bruno won't need to have it bathed in salt water, which probably stings a bit. He definitely doesn't like it'. Bruno isn't stupid. When he saw me with a bowl in one hand and the salt in the other, he would hide under the table or behind the chair – but I was relentless. I always found him. It's not easy to bathe a wart on the face of a reluctant dog when you only have two hands and the dog has teeth and isn't afraid to use them if pushed beyond endurance.

So it was a relief, for me at least, when Vet Zoe said that the time had come to remove the wart, with Vet Emily doing the surgery. Bruno, of course, had no idea what was to come …

I dropped him off with Vet Emily last Tuesday morning, bright and early. He was all happy and waggy tailed and pleased to see her again. If only he'd known, he might have been less waggy tailed and more snarly. It's said that we are the only animals who can anticipate future events or have an awareness of our own mortality. I'm not sure that's always true, but it's certainly true that Bruno wasn't anticipating any unpleasantness when I handed him over in the vet's car park on Tuesday morning.

I took Milly for a walk in the park. She wasn't happy. She very clearly wanted to know what I'd done with Bruno, but even though I told her that he was at the vet's and would be home at teatime, she wasn't happy. When we got home, she searched for Bruno all over the house, but of course she didn't find him. She dealt with her anxiety as she normally does and went to sleep.

Time passed. More time passed. And then a bit more time passed. It felt like a long day. But then, around 2.30 pm, Vet Emily phoned. Bruno's op had gone well. The wart had been easy to remove and not deep rooted. Bruno had been fine with the anaesthetic and was coming round nicely. His blood tests and ultrasound scan had shown nothing untoward. Emily would send tissue samples off for analysis, just to be on the safe side, but felt pretty confident that there was no malignancy and that this was just a wart. Phew! And I could collect him at 4.40 pm I should expect him to be quite drowsy after the anaesthetic, so he'd probably sleep most of the time once I got him home ...

Off I went again to the vet's, to do the same doggy handover in the car park that I'd done in the morning, but this time in reverse. The nurse brought Bruno out, together with his pain killers and surgical pack. 'He's been very chirpy,' she said, 'but he'll probably go to sleep once he gets home.' Bruno clearly wasn't listening.

One thing was different. As Bruno emerged from the vet's surgery, I could see that firmly fixed around his neck was the Cone of Shame ... The nurse repeated what Emily had said earlier, that Bruno needed to wear the Elizabethan collar (AKA Buster collar, AKA Cone of Shame) for two weeks, to stop him scratching the wound and opening it up or causing infection. Two weeks! Two weeks is quite a long time when you are a little dog who is being forced to wear an implement of torture ...

As soon as we got home, Bruno greeted Milly quite perfunctorily, and then went into the kitchen and demanded food – and then some more food. And then, since he will NOT poo in the garden, we had to go for a walk round the block so he could do what he needed to do in the rainy darkness of the street.

I confidently expected that once we returned home, Bruno would find a warm and comfortable spot and go to sleep. That's what the vet and the nurse expected, too. Bruno didn't know or care what we expected, and he had his own agenda to pursue.

Pursue it he did, for much of the night. Round and round the house he went, trying to rid himself of the Cone of Shame. Rubbing up against the wall didn't help; hooking it round the corner of the ottoman didn't help; squeezing through a narrow space just meant he got stuck. The collar remained in place whatever he did.

Milly took herself off at bedtime and went to the back of her crate, where Bruno never ventures, and went to sleep. Bruno dozed for a few minutes, then barked, then got up and tried to think of a new way to remove the dreaded cone. Then he'd doze, bark, try to remove the collar, and so on, all through the night. Then, around 5 am, he decided that enough was enough for tonight, settled himself on his dog bed, and went to sleep. I'd have liked to do the same, but at 6.30 am Milly wanted to go into the garden for a wee. And then I had to get up. April, the dog walker, now restored to us with the easing of Lockdown, was coming at 9 am to take Milly for a walk, and my shopping was due to be delivered shortly thereafter.

Bruno seemed quite outraged when April left without him. Whatever could she be thinking of? Only some more of the post-surgery special food could assuage his hurt feelings, and then we needed our quick flip round the block so he could perform his toilet to his satisfaction. Then he went to sleep until Milly came home.

I think he told her all about his day at the vet's. Certainly they had their heads together for a time and seemed to be deep in communication of some kind. Then both dogs had another sleep, and then it was time for more food, Bruno's painkillers, and another brief walk around the block for you-know-what, and then home.

Bruno had another nap, and I felt hopeful that he'd accepted the Elizabethan collar. Wrong! As the evening progressed, he tried all the ways of removing it that he'd tried the night before, and some more that hadn't occurred to him earlier. And, of course, nothing worked. At least, nothing worked as far as removing the Elizabethan collar was concerned. Bruno's strategies were extremely effective at keeping me awake, though that was probably not his intention. He'd established early on that all the doggy pleading in the world and all the yipping he could manage would not succeed in persuading me to remove the collar. So he wasn't trying to keep me awake – but the law of unintended consequences dictated that he kept me awake anyway.

And that has been the pattern of our days and nights since Tuesday. Bruno cat naps (dog naps?) during the day, but devotes much of his waking time to devising new ways to destroy the collar. He's failed so far – but it is starting to look a bit bashed and battered. When I took him for a post-operative check with the vet on Thursday night, she gave me another collar to have in reserve, because we both agreed that the existing collar might not survive for 14 whole days … I've left it out of sight in the car until I need it. I suspect that if it was in the house, Bruno might try to eat it.

Bruno seems to be recovering well from his op. His wound seems clean and his appetite and other bodily functions are all normal. He's even shown some interest, not much, in his toys, especially the squeaky pink pig.

Today is Saturday, 19 December in the Year of the Pandemic 2020. Bruno is asleep right now, tired from all the thinking and planning he's been doing to devise ways to obliterate the dreaded Cone of Shame. Ten more days to go … the cone can come off on 29 December.

I don't know whether Bruno can anticipate future events. I've told him it's only ten more sleeps until the collar comes off, but I don't think he was listening. I can anticipate future events, though, and it will be a really happy moment for me as well as for Bruno when I can finally remove the cone and consign it to the dustbin. And get some sleep …

Is it appropriate to say Merry Christmas in the middle of a pandemic? I'm not sure, so I'm saying it anyway. Let's hope for better things in 2021. As Charles Dickens says in the closing words of *A Christmas Carol*, 'God bless us, Every one!'.

Bruno and the Cone of Shame (2)

The last time I wrote about Bruno was on 19 December, 2020. It's now 7 February, 2021. One of the things I said on 19 December was 'Ten more days to go ... the cone can come off on 29 December'. Oh dear! Remember that proverb about not counting your chickens until they are hatched?

Bruno did well up until Christmas Day – his wound seemed to be healing, he was eating and pooping and sleeping all as usual. On Christmas Day he was a little restless and grumpy through the day, but then, very late that night, everything changed. Bruno was still, of course, wearing the dreaded Cone of Shame which, let me remind you, had to stay in place until 29 December. So near, and yet so far ...

All that night, Bruno crashed around the house, trying to pull the collar off or, failing that, trying to rub his face (and his wound!) against anything he could reach – the corners of furniture, the edge of his toybox, anything. When that failed, he just lay down and whimpered until, rested a little bit, he raised himself from the dog bed and began crashing around again. It was distressing to watch Bruno. It must have been even more distressing to *be* Bruno. This was hugely different from his previous attempts to remove the hated cone – he seemed much more frantic, more distraught, and his energies now seemed directed at attacking his wound.

Nobody got any sleep. Well, Milly, bored with all the drama, took herself off into the garden room, pulled a cushion down on to the floor behind my chair and turned her back on the world. Bruno and I stayed in the living room, waiting for the morning to come … It was a long night.

Eventually, exhausted by all the crashing about, Bruno went to sleep on his dog bed. I was able to look at his wound, which looked red and angry. I was even able to take a photograph. 6 am. I let Milly out for a wee, made coffee and phoned the emergency vet.

'Send us the photo,' they said. So I did. Bruno was still sleeping. Milly was still hiding. I was still drinking coffee.

The vet phoned. He had a kind and reassuring voice. 'You don't need to bring Bruno in,' he said, 'but you do need to take him back to your own vet on Monday. In the meantime, keep him warm, give him painkillers and ring us back if you're worried. Send another photo tomorrow and we'll see if anything has changed.'

Boxing Day passed, as days do. Why is it called 'Boxing' Day, I wonder? Bruno was still restless and agitated, though his wound didn't look any different. I could show you the photos, but I won't. They are not pretty. You'd just go, 'yuck'. It was a long day. And an even longer night. Whatever was bothering Bruno seemed to bother him much more in the middle of the night. Have you ever noticed that yourself? That if you don't feel well, you often feel worse when everyone else is asleep and the house is quiet? Milly disappeared – I lost sight of her sometime around 10 pm and didn't see her again until she wanted to go for a wee at 6 am. I made coffee again. Took the photo. Sent it to the emergency vet. They phoned. No change. Take him back to Vet Emily tomorrow. More crashing about. More no sleep. It's all a bit of a blur, really. And the Cone of Shame hung around Bruno's neck. From my point of view, it was protecting him and stopping him from doing himself more damage. From his point of view, it was torture. I, who was supposed to be his friend, was torturing him. Bruno wasn't happy. Milly wasn't happy. I wasn't happy. Another day passed, and another night of crashing about and whimpering (it might have been me doing some of the whimpering).

Monday dawned. 28 December. We'd expected Bruno to be all healed and out of the Cone of Shame, AKA Elizabeth Collar, AKA Buster Collar, AKA implement of torture, on 29 December. We had to face facts. The Cone was going nowhere …

I emailed all the photos (Bruno's wound in close-up and technicolour!) to the vet, with an explanation of all that had happened. By this time, Bruno was shifting from sleep to crashing around trying to scratch the wound, now swollen and beginning to ooze pus. He struggled to get the collar off, and, on failing, shifted again to lying in a heap and whimpering, then going outside and scratching up the pebbles, as if the icy cold on his paws gave him some relief.

The vet phoned. 'We need to see him. Bring him up this morning'. Off we went to do the socially distanced doggy handover again. Milly and I sat in the car and waited. And waited. If we have to have a pandemic, cars and mobile phones do help us get through. I thought about how tough it must be for people who don't have the things that helped ease my life, and Bruno's. The rain hammered down on the car roof. Time passed.

I'll give you the short version of what the vet said when she phoned. Bruno's ears were inflamed, so she'd started treatment for that – his ears were probably painful, so that would be one reason for his distress. The main reason, though, was that he'd developed a 'suture reaction'. I'd never heard of a 'suture reaction' – have you?

It's no fun at all. Apparently, anyone having surgery – dogs, cats, horses, people, camels, lions, anyone – can develop a suture reaction. It's an allergic reaction to the sutures used to stitch up an incision, and it causes intense itching and pain. It can lead to infection. At worst, you might need another operation to remove and replace the sutures, but this was best avoided if possible. The bottom line was that we might have to 'tough it out' for the six to eight weeks it would take for the sutures to dissolve and the wound to heal … Bruno definitely needed pain relief. He might also need antibiotics. He had to keep the Cone of Shame for AS LONG AS IT TOOK FOR THE WOUND TO HEAL!!! It wasn't coming off on 29 December, or 30 or 31 … or, in fact, in January …

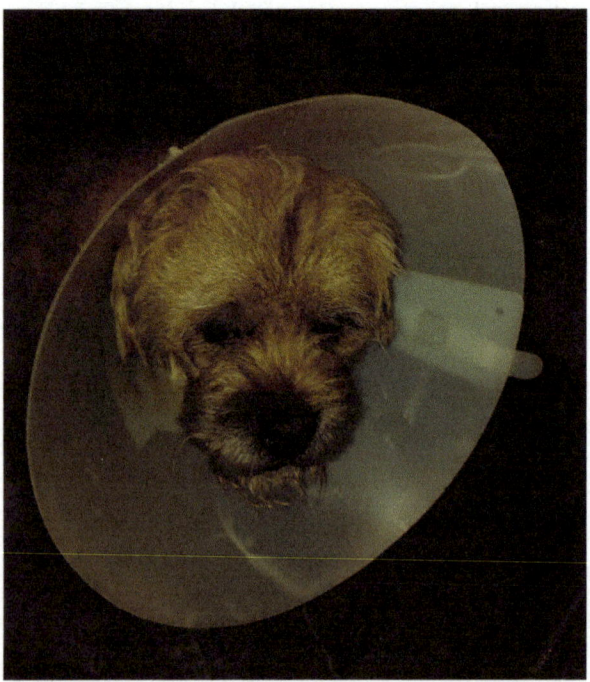

Bruno, still in the Cone of Shame and NOT happy.

The Adventures of Bruno

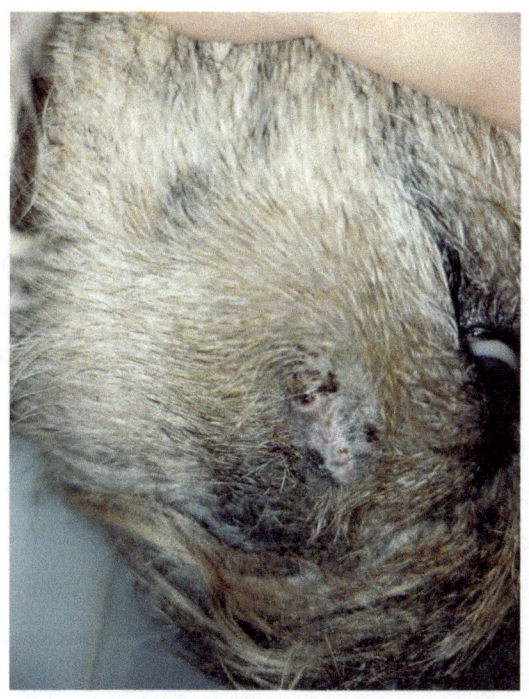

I know I said I wouldn't show you Bruno's suture reaction.
I lied. But this is one of the less gruesome pictures
(and I've deleted the others!)

Vet Emily went on to say that it was quite unusual for there to be a suture reaction, but then I think we both had the same thought in the same second. 'If it's going to happen,' she added, 'it will happen to Bruno ...'. Deep sighs all round, as we prepared for the long haul of the next few weeks ...

I'll spare you the details. Imagine lots of photos being taken and sent to the vet, and lots of phone calls telling me to take him up to the surgery. Imagine more socially distanced doggy handovers in the car park. Imagine an infection worsening and antibiotics being prescribed … and more antibiotics. Imagine that all Bruno's crashing about meant that the dreaded Cone rubbed a sore place on his neck, so the vet padded the collar with cotton wool and surgical tape to stop it from doing any more damage to Bruno's skin. And prescribed his second lot of pink antibiotics, which he'd been taking with reluctance up to now … I did tell him that fastening him into the Cone of Shame and feeding him his medication was almost as painful for me as it was for him, but I could tell that he didn't believe me.

This was the point where Bruno went on strike and learned, for the first time in his long life, that he has TEETH that can be used for other purposes than chewing food … They can, for example, be aimed at treacherous humans who torture you and then try to poison you by hiding noxious tablets in sausages, and cheese, and mackerel pate and anything else I could find. Bruno was having none of it. At first he ate the sausage or whatever but spat out the tablet. Then he refused to take any food from me. Then he tried to bite me. Three times. We had some extremely low moments.

Back to the vet. A new antibiotic, smaller and easier to disguise. More pain relief. More ear treatment. Ear drops. Another bite (luckily he got my sleeve, not my flesh). More trips to the vet. By the end of January, Bruno had seen (several times) Vet Zoe, Vet Emily, Vet Laura, Vet Ruth and Vet Alison, not to mention the veterinary nurses who brought him back to my car. And so the days passed, some more easily than others … and the nights. We did get some sleep, some nights. January prepared to leave … Bruno finished his last lot of medication on 3 February, and had an appointment – another one! – with Vet Laura on 4 February … This was seven weeks and two days from the date of his original surgery, so five weeks and two days after we'd expected to lose the Cone of Shame ... which now looked more than a bit battered and old (rather like me!).

There should now be a fanfare and a roll of drums. I sat patiently in my car, waiting for the nurse to bring Bruno back. Vet Laura phoned. 'Can you hear him?', she said. I could – he was yipping excitedly in the background. 'The wound is fully healed,' said Laura, 'and there's no infection. His ears are fine, too. He's done with the collar now – you can throw it away!' Imagine cheering and shouts and barks of joy ...

Bruno has now had three days without the Cone of Shame. He's almost happy to take bits of food from me again. I had sausages for tea last night. Bruno kept his distance at first, but gradually came closer, and closer – and yipped. 'Where's mine??' I gave him a bit of sausage and he took it with no hesitation at all. And there was nothing hidden inside. I wouldn't say he's forgiven me. He's a terrier, and terriers have long memories. They don't forget and they don't forgive. He will, however, put all the upsets and pain of the last seven weeks behind him and allow me to make amends with more sausage and longer walks ... His teeth are back to being used solely for chewing his dinner, and his toys and Milly's ball. He watched as I cut the Cone of Shame into pieces and put it in the bin in the kitchen, and then watched as I took the kitchen rubbish out to the dustbin. Had it really gone? It looked that way. Bruno went to sit on the ottoman in the conservatory, and watched the bin closely. The lid stayed shut, the Cone of Shame where it belonged – in the rubbish.

Home from the vet's, the cone vanquished …

The Adventures of Bruno

When the day is nearly over, and the dogs and I are sitting quietly in the living room, I sometimes notice Bruno watching me intently, and I wonder what is going through his mind ... Is he imagining uprising and revolution? Turning the tables on vets, and nurses and humans in general, and inventing a Cone of Shame for people? It's not impossible ...

Bruno Today: Postscript

Well, here we are, Wednesday, 28 April, 2021 – still living in Lockdown Land but slowly beginning to emerge into a new and changed world. Like Bruno, I'm fairly old now, so have had both doses of the coronavirus vaccine, and am well-accustomed to mask-wearing and social distancing. We never expected to be living through a pandemic, but life is always unpredictable. We do what we can do to keep ourselves and other people as safe as it's possible to be. The dogs and I walk round the lake once more, and Bruno once again can look forward to outings with April, who can walk further and faster than I can. Bruno and Milly aren't quite sure what's going on – Milly occasionally growls at people she knows when they are wearing a mask – but we all get on with life as best we can, day by day by day. We know how lucky we are, all things considered.

Bruno's face has now healed fully, and you can see only the tiniest scar if you look very closely. He's happy to take food from me again – especially if I'm having sausages for tea. He doesn't run about quite as much as he used to do, (nor do I and nor does Milly) but he takes the same interest as ever in wall weeing and stealing Milly's toys. We had another all too close encounter with fox poo a month or so ago, but I will spare you any detailed description. It's enough to say that what happened before happened again, right down to the fox poo concealed in the bushes, the car ride and the shower(s). I have a secret weapon now, though. Emily and Emily's mum sent me a special fox poo-removing shampoo for my birthday – and it works! I only had to shower Bruno twice this time.

The Adventures of Bruno

And so we go on, survivors (so far!) of the coronavirus pandemic. We enjoy our small day-to-day pleasures, and Bruno knows that we will have a trip to a beach as soon as it is safe and sensible to do so. We enjoy our garden visits with friends, though Bruno was a bit cross when I didn't give him any of the clotted cream scones Emily and her mum brought on their visit last Saturday. I explained that clotted cream scones aren't good for little dogs, and gave him one of his little bone-shaped treats instead. It was acceptable. Adequate. He took it. And only glumped a little bit ...

We are still here, which is surely something to celebrate, and we may all have a few more adventures left in us yet. Bruno certainly thinks so! Watch this space!

THE END (for now)

Bruno in a Happy Place …

The Adventures of Bruno

Bruno and Milly on the Ottoman in the Garden Room

Bruno, Milly & Annie in a Happy Place